Cu

Trumps Strategy

Achieving high performance through people

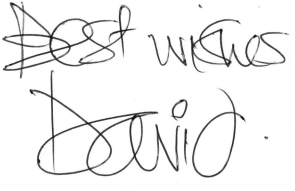

David Smith

**Grosvenor House
Publishing Limited**

The right of David Smith to be identified as the author of this
work has been asserted in accordance with Section 78
of the Copyright, Designs and Patents Act 1988

The book cover picture is copyright to David Smith

This book is published by
Grosvenor House Publishing Ltd
Link House
140 The Broadway, Tolworth, Surrey, Kt6 7Ht.
www.grosvenorhousepublishing.co.uk

A CIP record for this book
is available from the British Library

ISBN 978-1-78623-934-1

AUTHOR OF 'ASDA MAGIC – THE 7 PRINCIPLES OF BUILDING A HIGH PERFORMANCE CULTURE' 2011 – GROSVENOR HOUSE PUBLISHING

TESTIMONIALS FOR 'ASDA MAGIC'

- "David – I have just read your book, and wanted to say thank you. I have read it cover to cover. It served as an epiphany to some of the situations I have experienced at work, and given me some closure on lots of the issues I have to wrestle with – it is an excellent read."

- "Just wanted to let you know that I read your book, and it was an excellent reminder of my development from young manager to mature leader. I laughed, I cried – it was like living the journey of my life and all my values again. It made me realise how lucky I was to have experienced such an amazing culture."

- "Thank you, write another." (Well here is another for you!!)

- "This book was absolutely brilliant. I have read many other management/business books before, and this one is one of the best, if not the best. Smith cuts out all the management 'buzz' words and says it in plain English. The book is clear, concise, easy to read, and everything is to the point. Smith addresses key areas including communication, leadership, listening to colleagues, managing talent and creating a working environment which makes people enjoy their work. All these areas are backed up with real life experience and results. While the book is based on Smith's experience of working for Asda over 15 years, all of the 7 principles covered in 'Asda Magic' can be applied to any retail environment."

- "I really enjoyed reading this book. Such an easy read, and full of great stories to bring the thinking to life. It's an outstanding read for anyone looking to improve the culture in their own business. Whether it's a multinational company, a small business, or just within your own team at work – this book has great food for thought on the things you can do to make a difference. David Smith has managed to cram inspiration into every chapter – not just with his own thought, but from many of the old executive team who helped turn the business around. In short, if you're looking for a book full of dozens of ideas on improving your culture in your business? Well in supermarket terms, this is the One-Stop Shop!"

- "David Smith's rather splendid biography of Asda shows us how an inspiring customer and staff-centric vision created extraordinary results from ordinary people. What looked like alchemy in turning round the so nearly insolvent Asda turns out to be captured in just 7 principles. Better still Asda's leaders motivate and communicate to bring out the best in their colleagues. Smith has in fact given us a BOGOF here. We have a biography of Asda and a thoughtful distillation of just what saved a business so near the rocks that you wonder why on earth Archie Norman took the Chief Executive challenge. Smith looks at retail leadership from all angles. We know that retail, above all styles of commerce, is based on great people; in stores and in leadership. It does take your breath away to see just how many leaders Asda has produced. Archie and Allan Leighton were clearly obsessed by recruiting A* people and inculcating their Asda culture. It is also clear that

Asda became a very self-critical business: 'never sat-isfied with current performance'. Perhaps we should all be paranoid. It is a coup for Smith that in every chapter he has reflections from those Asda alumni: King, Baker, deNunzio, Mason, Bond, Cheesewright. Marvellous. But best of all, Smith lays out his case for Retail management that involved thousands of modestly paid colleagues, in a business that faced much better financed, stronger competitors. And he is bang on when he observes that few businesses are blessed with the opportunity of near bankruptcy, and the momentum that brings in terms of a force for change. Most practically, Asda underpinned its execution and 'everyday low costs' – thus delivering a performance culture in store that was never going to be a job for consultants."

DEDICATION

I dedicate this second business book to my wonderful wife Liz – who has been with me – and put up with my foibles – for 4 decades now. That has been worth more than I can say in words!

CHAPTER 1

Preamble –
Why Write A Second Book?

> "Colleagues should take care of each other, have fun, celebrate success, learn by failure, look for reasons to praise not criticise, communicate freely, and respect each other." Richard Branson

My first book 'Asda Magic – the 7 principles of building a high performance culture' was a case study of the turnaround of a retail business, involving its people and culture.

I have received a storm of positive feedback from people who worked in the Asda business during that period and, interestingly, also from many business executives and commentators who have little or no connection to the Asda turnaround story. The positive feedback which most surprised me regarding 'Asda Magic', came from far flung countries around the world and people who have never worked in retail businesses.

To all of you who enjoyed 'Asda Magic', found practical value from it – especially those who were kind enough to say it was the "best business book they have ever read".......................my sincere thanks to you all.

You have inspired me to write a second – some have requested a second – so in all respects this second book is down to you!!

KEEPING IT SHORT AND TO THE POINT

That preamble presents a dilemma. How do you face into that difficult 'Second Album'? Musicians who produce a brilliant first album often fail to produce their second.

I have been thinking for some time about responding to the various requests to "write another book". A 'sequel' to any business book is a tough call. One thing I have learned, in this age of Twitter, is that any business book needs to be shorter, rather than longer. I need to say what I have to say and then shut up – or you the readers are not going to finish it!

Whilst in corporate life, I developed a practice of summarising business books I was reading, and sharing those handwritten summaries with executive colleagues. I found that people really valued those short 'pithy' summaries.................because it saved them the daunting task of ploughing through a textbook. We are all busy people with lives which are full. There are too many emails to deal with – too many reports to digest. Reading business books, no matter how highly recommended.................is a chore.

I remember when Jim Collins published 'Good to Great'...........it became a must read of its day. My CEO at that time was keen that leaders in the business should read it............and they knew they ought to read it. For those who hadn't made time – they devoured my summary of it with great relish. Key points made easy!

Book summaries became something that a variety of providers made commercially available..............and these became compulsory reading for busy executives – a shorthand for keeping abreast of new thinking and research – without wading through even more text.

Our attention span, in this age when we are overwhelmed with information, has become ever shorter. Consequently, I want to respond to this and make this book a quick and easy read. This is not an academic tome, but a practitioner's book, with personal observations about real businesses – again told through storytelling.

THE 7 PRINCIPLES OF BUILDING A HIGH PERFORMANCE CULTURE

In my first book, I explored the premise of 7 principles for building a high performance culture. For ease of your memory, these were:-

<u>Hiring for attitude/training for skill</u> - the attitude of the people you hire is a huge signal about your culture, and the only valid predictor of 'fit'.

<u>Communicate/communicate/communicate</u> – it is our responsibility as leaders to inspire our people. The more they know the more they will care. Great communication is the 'rocket fuel' of cultural change.

<u>Listening</u> – systematically listening to your people – giving them voice to comment about what is and what is not working is the highest form of respect you can show to your people.

<u>Choosing an appropriate style of leadership</u> – leadership matters! We all know people leave poor leaders, rather than organisations. My observation is that a command and control style of leadership is still alive and well in many organisations today..........and it is definitely counterproductive. Organisations need to choose a leadership style which is appropriate to the modern world and taps into the discretionary effort of those being led – rather than switching it off.

<u>Managing people's performance – dealing with under-performance and pushing talent</u> – this is an area that most CEOs admit to be their hardest leadership challenge – yet shying away from this is a definite workforce 'turn off' and demotivator. Employees want to see you dealing with this effectively.

<u>Recognition</u> – we are obsessed with the management and maximization of effective remuneration. At the same time, we naturally under play recognition. The simplest 'thank you', is extremely powerful in recognising people's efforts – and shows real respect for those contributing to our overall success in an organisation. Because recognition is 'free' it is under rated by many in leadership roles.

<u>Creating a fun workplace and a sense of community</u> – work which is made fun gets done better. Allowing

people to enjoy working together in teams – giving them permission to have fun – and to bring their whole self into their role, is one of the keys to people giving of their discretionary effort.

INGREDIENTS OF THE HIGH PERFORMANCE 'CAKE MIX'

Those 7 principles were my observations about the key 'ingredients' of the cultural turnaround at Asda over a 15 year period.

My business life now involves a 'portfolio' of business speaking; consulting in organisations and mentoring CEOs and other executives. Having spent a good number of years now, working with organisations in all business sectors, and all sizes, in different countries...
......I now realise that these 7 principles are generic to 'baking the cake' of a high performance culture.

People are people, wherever they work, in a small family firm in the construction industry, or in a large multinational FMCG business. Whatever the context, people desire some basic elements in the culture of the organisation, in order to be able to perform at their best.

EXAMPLES AND STORIES WHICH ARE 'NOT THE USUAL SUSPECTS'

This short book seeks to illustrate that the 7 principles occur in high performance cultures in many different contexts. I believe people are somewhat tired of hearing about the culture at Apple or Google. Most businesses do not live in the Global Tech bubble, and there has been too much written about these businesses already.

My aim is to use less well known examples and stories from businesses which exemplify great culture and high performance. I'm going to try to steer away from 'the usual suspects'.

LEADERSHIP BEHAVIOUR AFFECTS RESULTS

I believe that engaging people and building a high performance culture has a massive impact on business results – and on the well-being of the people within the business. This is a truly win-win agenda for the organisation and for the employees. I also disagree with the cynics who believe that the engagement of employees is merely a passing fad.

In the world of today, employers who consistently ignore the needs of their people, who think their business is all about product or innovation – will ultimately underperform in the long run.

I will seek to demonstrate, by the use of less well known examples, that the simple principles of the Asda turnaround case study really do have powerful effect in other contexts.

COMMON SENSE IS AN OXYMORON

Many people have told me that my 7 principles are 'common sense'. I would agree that there is no rocket science here. However, I believe that common sense may be something of an oxymoron. Common sense, in my experience, can be exceedingly rare!! Leaders know many of these 7 common sense principles. They know they should inspire their people in the way they communicate – but in the cut and thrust they send out yet another email. They know they should get employees voice on what is working. They know they should be taking time to notice outperformance and to recognise it. However, in the real world, events intervene. We get busy. Urgent business priorities pile up. There are things we have to do and cannot avoid – and they eat up our time.

This is the reason we don't often enact these 'common sense' things which build and sustain a high performance culture. It's not because we don't believe they matter – they just fall down the hierarchy of priorities.

WHY ARE PEOPLE FEELING NEGATIVE ABOUT THEIR EMPLOYERS?

Gallup, the international survey organization, is constantly producing data which illustrates that only 30% of people are fully engaged with their employer's business.

Some global figures go so far as to suggest that only 13% of people are fully engaged with their work, and only 20% trust their leaders to tell the truth about difficult issues. Trust is a huge issue in many sectors, with some surveys showing that 70% of employees don't trust their immediate boss. Taken together, these survey figures are both significant and concerning.

The Office of National Statistics survey of wellbeing in 2011 found that people are very happy with their children and family life – but much less so with their working life. Perhaps the fact that relationships in our personal lives are more open, informed and satisfying, illustrates that people are also wanting similar things in their working lives.

DISCRETIONARY EFFORT – THE HOLY GRAIL OF HIGH PERFORMANCE

There is now a plethora of research available, which shows a high degree of correlation between engaged employees and levels of productivity. It is clear that people will only give discretionary effort when they are engaged by the environment in which they are working. This involves belief in the mission and purpose of the enterprise, and the way they are being inspired and made to feel that their contribution counts. You cannot pressure people to give more for less – your people have to want to go the extra mile for you.

THE IMPORTANCE OF BUILDING TRUST

One of my 7 principles, in particular, is key to building trust. Great leaders must communicate/communicate/communicate honestly (face to face preferably) in order to ensure that people feel totally part of the bigger picture. They also need to be given voice to come back with their own views. We have to listen to them and respond.

In my experience, people will always appreciate and recognise honesty when they see it. Most employees want to be a part of the solution – whatever the problem/ situation – so open dialogue always helps people to feel valued.

I have seen many examples where employees have the answer...............if managers just take the time to listen to their voice and talk to them.

I very much concur with Richard Branson's thoughts from the quote at the beginning of this chapter. Leaders/ CEOs do need to foster a culture where "colleagues take care of each other.....have fun.....celebrate success..... communicate freely and respect each other." They have proven a winner for Richard in Virgin. These things are the building blocks of a great culture – they are not just 'nice to have'. They may be common sense actions, but they are the building blocks of a high performance culture

If culture really does trump strategy..................... then what is it? I will answer that question for you in the next chapter.

CHAPTER 2

If Culture Trumps Strategy – What Is Culture?

"Culture eats strategy for breakfast" Peter Drucker

"The thing I have learned at IBM is that culture is everything" Louis Gerstner

"If you get the culture right, most of the other stuff will take care of itself" Tony Hsieh CEO Zappos

"Culture can become a 'secret weapon' that makes extraordinary things happen" Jon Katzenbach Booz & Co

"Engagement is not a survey....it's not a popularity contest....it's not a HR activity....it's a leadership activity......measured through the line" Archie Norman Chairman ITV

"You can have all the right strategy in the world; if you don't have the right culture, you're dead" Patrick Whitesell CEO WME

"Culture is about performance, and making people feel good about how they contribute to the whole." Tracy Streckenbach

**I HAVE NO DOUBT – HOW PEOPLE FEEL
AFFECTS PERFORMANCE**

In giving this book the title 'Culture trumps Strategy',
I have nailed my colours to the mast...................
engagement and culture are clearly linked to business
performance. To me, it has always seemed obvious that
the way a workforce feels about their place of work will
materially affect the performance of that organisation.
This is especially true of service organisations, where
customers are at the 'receiving end' of good or bad
service. But it is also relevant where businesses make
products or exist for other purposes. You only have to
look to past examples such as British Leyland, where a
disillusioned workforce were sleeping on the night shift,
to realise that a disastrous culture will inevitably lead
to massive underperformance and decline.

Contrast that with Nissan's Sunderland plant, which
runs one of the most productive car manufacturing
processes in the world, and you can see how differing
cultures produce very different results. If you are interested in how the culture was intentionally built at
Nissan's Sunderland plant – Peter Wickens book 'The
Ascendant Organisation' is a fascinating case study.
Needless to say, that high performance culture did not
happen by accident.

Culture always trumps strategy – I'm with Peter Drucker
on that – and there are many case studies to back up
that point of view. I want to introduce a few examples
to you as this book unfolds.

WHAT IS THIS SLIPPERY CONCEPT – CULTURE?

Organisational cultures shape the way things are done in organisations. Peter Honey articulates a simple formula: what people can do, plus what they want to do, added to what they think they are allowed to do equals what they do.

In bad cultures the can do's (skills and talents) and the want to do's (willingness and motivation) are limited by the allowed to do's, both real and imagined. Dr Edwards Deming said "put good people into a bad system and the system always wins."

BAD CULTURE

The worst cultures are where management defines a set of values and behaviours...............often beautifully written up on wall charts..........but conversation at the water cooler or coffee station tells you the real culture isn't like that at all.

WHAT ARE PEOPLE LIKE WHEN
THE BOSS ISN'T AROUND?

The consultants would define culture as 'the way things get done around here'.

My refinement to that would be that culture is what happens when the boss isn't around. How do people behave in an organisation when no one in authority can see them? How do leaders behave when the CEO isn't around? It makes perfect sense to me that your people can make you or break you..............and that always comes down to culture. Culture really does count ....it is critical to success.

CULTURE 'LEAKS' OUT

The thing we should quickly realise, is that culture 'leaks out' to customers and suppliers. This can either be extremely positive or extremely negative. I remember a particularly poignant example of this from a few years ago. I was travelling on a train to speak for a client. When travelling fairly long distances, I usually get up from my seat about 15 minutes before my journey ends, in order to gather my things, and stretch my legs. I'm usually dashing off to my appointment, so I like to go to the end of the carriage I'm travelling in, and get ready to alight from the train.

On this particular journey, there were two railway employees standing chatting in the same vestibule at the end of my carriage. Their conversation, which was quite loud and boisterous, was about how bad the new food offer on the train was. They told me that head office didn't know what they were doing, the pricing was wrong and the quality was poor. Well, they didn't actually tell me, they were telling each other.............but I couldn't help overhearing their loud conversation. Not a great impression so far! Culture leaks out.

We were now about 10 minutes from my destination station, and their conversation, still extremely loud, ranged onto their shift patterns. One asked the other how many early starts he had experienced that week. Apparently one of these guys had two earlies, whilst the other had four. They then had a long 'rant' about how terrible the scheduling and roster system was. Again, head office came in for a verbal bashing.....not knowing what they were doing......again!!

We were now 5 minutes from the termination of the train, and a lot more passengers were gathering their things and entering the vestibule, in preparation for getting off the train. Still the loud discourse from our two guys went on!! By now they were castigating the railway promotion system. Apparently, they wanted to get out of catering and become train guards......a promotion needing some sort of assessment centre. They told the gathered passengers, who couldn't fail to be listening to this loud exchange...............how they had both been to the assessment centre twice, and both had failed. They railed about how unfair it was, and the fact that the guy running the process was useless.

You can imagine my perception of the management, and the relationship with employees of this particular railway business by now. Not great....to say the least! Culture leaks out......in this case to the severe detriment of the reputation of the business. So, as we pulled into the end of the line, and I had my conference to get to.........
...........the customer who had waited first in line to get off the train..........had to wait whilst these two rather 'bad example' employees casually ambled off the train first.....blocking the exit and ignoring their customers.

A CULTURE WHICH GETS THINGS DONE WILLINGLY & WELL

During my 15 years working at Asda, we worked very hard to build a culture which was centred around the aim of 'getting things done willingly and well, through others'. This aim embraces what Peter Honey was driving at. What people actually do is a mix of what they can do, what they want to do and what they feel they are allowed to do.

As an example of the kind of culture which was achieved, in terms of 'getting things done willingly and well', let me relate another story. One great idea in the Asda Retail business where I worked, was to invite suppliers and consultants to come and work in the stores in the few weeks running up to Christmas. Readers will know that food retailers experience a huge spike in sales volume in that period, and that every pair of hands is valuable. It also gave those suppliers a valuable insight into the internal workings of the Asda business and culture.

I well remember one of the leadership development consultants we used at Asda sharing his experience with me. He had spent a couple of days in an Asda store, and was extremely complimentary about the whole experience. He told me how incredibly busy the store had been, and he had been working with the team on fresh produce. I think he had spent a couple of days filling fixtures with sprouts and carrots. The thing which had impressed him about the culture was twofold. Firstly, he was impressed by the good humour of the colleagues he worked alongside – both with each other – and with customers. Secondly, he was amazed by how concerned the produce team was to ensure that he was ok. As the new boy on the team, they kept asking whether he knew what he was doing, and were concerned to check that he was coping with the pressure – despite being rushed off their feet. As a consultant, he was experiencing the culture of the business first hand – and finding it vibrant, helpful and above all fun.

Interestingly, he contrasted that with a work experience from early in his working life. As an undergraduate, he had worked in a local hospital 30 years previously. He recounted being asked to sweep a corridor as part of his duties. Whilst undertaking this simple task, he was approached by a number of his full time colleagues and told to "slow down" – since he was working much faster than their normal pace. They told him "slow down young man – we have to work here regularly and we pace ourselves differently". How devastating for a young student to be told he was too fast!

Culture leaks out to other fellow employees and to customers – and that can either be a good or a poor experience – but you cannot stop the culture leaking.

THE EFFECT OF CULTURE ON PERFORMANCE IS 'MASSIVE'

Culture is key to success or failure. Culture cannot fail to leak out. Culture can be 'felt', and its effects can be seen and experienced. Culture materially affects performance.

I spend a lot of my working portfolio speaking with CEOs and MDs of businesses. Whenever I ask them about their views on the effect of culture upon performance, they invariably use the term 'massive'. I believe they are right – otherwise I wouldn't be writing this book. The personal experience of these business leaders is that the cultural norms of the organisation affect employee performance to a 'massive' degree.

I was looking at a 2015 survey of 90,000 employees, employed in a variety of sectors, carried out in 19 different countries. Of those 90,000 employees surveyed, only 20% were fully engaged believers in the culture that they worked in.....................meaning 80% were not fully engaged (that's classic Pareto 80/20) ....a sobering statistic. Of the 80% - 40% responded that they were moderately engaged, and 40% said they were totally disengaged with the businesses they worked for. It is a sad fact that there are substantial numbers of people working for businesses they neither like nor believe in. I'm sure we've all worked with people who seem to take delight in constantly criticising their employer and the culture – yet remain there for substantial chunks of their working lives. That is not good for their well-being, nor for the performance of the businesses they work in.

The key statistic from that survey of 90,000 employees which really backs up what CEOs think anecdotally is that the 20% who are fully engaged in their culture – are 85% better at giving great service to customers, and 96% better at coming up with ideas/innovation to improve the business. That is a 'massive' differentiator of performance, and it therefore must be worth building a culture in which a high percentage of your people really believe in the business and are highly engaged with the mission and purpose.

WORKING ON YOUR BUSINESS/ORGANISATION CULTURE

Is it worth working on improving organisational culture to get 'massive' improvement in the performance of your people? I think the answer to that question is a resounding affirmative.

The challenge, is that cultural change, in terms of building trust and positivity.....................is a long hard slog. Culture can go backwards very quickly in light of negative events, but positive building of a culture is tough.

Peter Cheese, Chief Executive of the Chartered Institute of People and Development, thinks that culture takes years to change. He believes that culture is not 'part of the game', it is 'the whole game'..............and that whilst we can change strategy very quickly, cultural change takes years to enact. I totally agree with him, and spent 15 years working on the culture at Asda. I like to think of positive steps in culture in terms of 5 year horizons.................because it takes that long to see substantial improvements.

CULTURE CAN EASILY DROP OFF THE BUSINESS AGENDA

My observation would be that few CEOs dispute that culture is important, but it often slips off the agenda due to other events and priorities. Leaders constantly have to respond to urgent matters and crises as they occur, and the day to day running of an organisation can be all consuming for even the best of executives.

Chris Brady, when he was Principal at Henley Management College, bemoaned the fact that there was so much evidence to illustrate the positive influence of a great culture, yet leaders still constantly said they were "too busy" to work on it. Events will blow you off course, unless you determine that you will allocate time and resource to building a strong culture.

CHAPTER 3

If The Effect Of Culture Appears 'Massive' – What's The Effect On The Bottom Line?

"High performing companies should be striving to create a great place for people to do great work" Marylyn Carlson

"Customers will never love a company unless the employees love it first" Simon Sinek

"I used to believe that culture was 'soft', and had little to do with the bottom line. What I believe today is that our culture is everything to do with our bottom line now and into the future" Vern Dosch – author 'Wired Differently'

EMPLOYEE ENGAGEMENT AND CULTURE – INEXORABLY LINKED

Discussion of the term employee engagement first appeared in the 2000s, and academics were somewhat sceptical at the time. Some said it was just a re-labelling of employee involvement. However, the term employee engagement has caught the imagination of CEOs. It made sense to many of them that their culture was important, and they were looking for ways to improve productivity, through engaging with their people.

The engaged employee understands the organisation, and 'gets' the bigger picture. The engaged employee is more likely to respect others, and go the extra mile for the organisation. This is a source of discretionary effort. Discretionary effort, given because people care, is the 'nirvana' for most CEOs who are switched on to the idea of improving culture. They are the business leaders who realise that this kind of vibrant culture, where people care, brings real business benefit, and is a great place for employees to work – it's a 'win-win'.

ERNST & YOUNG DATA – EMPLOYEE ENGAGEMENT/PERFORMANCE

Ernst & Young have quoted a large number of academic surveys, which point to the fact that the most engaged employees drive real business performance. Ernst & Young subsequently ran a major global survey within their own business units around the world. They found a clear strong correlation between the performance of the most engaged employees and brand favourability. Culture counts – even with accountants!

Ernst & Young also found 11% difference in the retention rates between the most engaged and least engaged business units. In EY, a gap equating to thousands of pounds sterling in hiring and induction costs. EY proved, through their own internal global data, that the current academic research trends, on the links between culture and performance are correct.

IT'S THE CULTURE STUPID! CULTURE REALLY DOES COUNT

It has always made sense to me that culture trumps strategy. Culture is the backdrop to every piece of business and organisational effort. How we feel about our company will affect how we perform. Discretionary effort is only given to organisations with positive cultures. Every sales negotiation, every routine task, every transaction with a customer – they all happen within a cultural context. The effect of that culture is massive.

Bad cultures will cause you to underperform. Great cultures will lift your performance beyond the norm. Are you a believer in the power of the culture, and the effect on the performance of your people? As I said, I don't have any difficulty with this intellectually, but you may need some examples to help persuade you.

PRÉT A MANGER – FOCUS ON CULTURE AT INDUCTION

Prét a Manger devotes as much time to building enthusiasm in their cultural inductions, as they spend time explaining the minutiae of how to serve the products to the customers. Prét thinks that enthusiasm in the culture is powerful.

STARBUCKS BELIEFS ABOUT ENGAGED PEOPLE

Starbucks founder Howard Schultz has famously talked about his belief that engaged people can elevate the customer experience. Schultz is a big believer in the power of the culture for results.

MARKS & SPENCER MEASURES ENGAGEMENT AND PERFORMANCE

Marks & Spencer has developed some robust methodology which quantifies the difference in sales growth between stores with high engagement/strong culture, and those where it is weaker – and can quantify the effect of engagement and culture on performance.

WHITBREAD – CORRELATION BETWEEN CULTURE AND PERFORMANCE

Whitbread is a company dedicated to building culture through the positive engagement of people. Whitbread has improved engagement scores by roughly 25% across different business units over a period of 3 years, and has found strong correlation between the best cultures by unit, and top financial performance. Whitbread would say that making their people happier in their workplace has been transformational in terms of actual performance. This phenomenon is at the heart of accessing discretionary effort and the willingness of people to go the extra mile for their employer.

SAINSBURY – A CULTURAL ENGAGEMENT STRATEGY

J. Sainsbury, whose CEO for 10 years was Justin King, and CMO was Mike Coupe (now CEO of Sainsbury himself) – both were ex Asda executives, and took much of the Asda cultural initiatives to Sainsbury. Sainsbury as a business became a great believer in the clear causal link between cultural engagement and sales performance. The executives leading the business knew this from their experience during the Asda cultural/ performance turnaround. They proved that these same cultural initiatives and principles contributed to 15% of each individual store growth in Sainsbury. Good cultural principles work in any context.

Justin King, the previous CEO of Sainsbury, said that their cultural engagement strategy had played an important part in halving employee turnover over a period of 5 years. He advocated strong cultural values, and relentless communication in driving the engagement of the people at Sainsbury.

NATIONAL DIFFERENCES SHOW THE UK LAGGING IN ENGAGEMENT

There is an abundance of strong evidence, in a wide variety of studies, that productivity is strongly linked to culture and engagement of employees regardless of sector. Organisations with high engagement outperform their peers in shareholder returns and margins. Employees who care will automatically want to innovate, add value and give of their discretionary effort to help the enterprise succeed.

The concern for UK organisations is that many surveys show the UK lagging behind other nations in terms of culture and engagement. We are 9th amongst the world's 12 largest economies for the engagement of employees. Surprisingly, we do not have the best cultures universally around businesses in the UK. Consequently, this must be part of the causal link for our productivity to be lagging behind..................indeed the UK's output is 15% below the average for the rest of the G7 industrialised nations – according the Office of National Statistics. On an 'output per worker' basis, the figure is even worse. Our UK productivity on that measure is 20% lower than the rest of the G7 nations in 2011.

A study by Kenexa estimated that the UK economy is missing out on £26billion revenue because of poor employee engagement and lacklustre cultures. 2/3 of the UK's 30 million workers are said to be disengaged, which means they are to some extent 'going through the motions' at work, and not exerting their full effort. Nor are they giving their best service, or deploying their innovative ideas and intelligence to their work.

This is a shameful set of statistics for the UK...... ....and is something leaders need to be addressing. If culture is 'massive' in performance terms.................and cultural disengagement is common............then the best leaders need an agenda for change.

EUROPE LAGS THE WORLD IN CULTURE AND PERFORMANCE

Studies also show, rather depressingly, that the UK is not alone with regard to lacklustre cultural performance. A 2013 survey by AON Hewitt showed that engagement levels within organisational cultures across Europe were behind the global average.

In Europe, 17% of employees surveyed were fully engaged, against a global average of 20%. The highest performing region globally was Latin America – with 32% fully engaged................a much more creditable performance.

If this causes you to despair for our own economy, there are even worse cultural results in the developing world. A recent Gallup survey in India revealed that only 9% of employees there were fully engaged in the businesses they worked for, and the company culture.

THE UK GOVERNMENT RESPONSE TO ENGAGEMENT AND CULTURE

The weight of this statistical evidence caused the UK Government to put its weight behind the 'Engage for Success' initiative, ably chaired by David McLeod. There have been too many failing cultures, such as the one widely reported in the Mid Staffordshire Health Trust. Their failure to build a culture which engaged employees led to higher mortality rates than the rest of the Health sector. In this context, it really was a matter of life and death. In hospitals around the country where the culture is better, and levels of employee engagement are higher, there is real evidence of lower mortality rates.

It is not only in the health sector where cultures have been shown to be toxic. There are a plethora of examples in the Banking sector, and culture could be said to be a major factor in the last major financial crisis, which triggered a worldwide recession.

The UK Government has acknowledged that culture does affect performance, and their encouragement of the methodology and work of the 'Engage for Success' initiative has reinforced this.

CULTURE NEEDS A PLAN OF ACTION

A survey called 'fulfilment @ work' in 2013 showed that 10 million people working in the UK are unfulfilled. Poor levels of job satisfaction and commitment drive both employee absence and intention to quit and find another job. All these factors fall through to bottom line performance. This should be no surprise. How you feel about your work directly affects how you perform. Culture directly impacts performance.

A further survey of 45,000 employees by the recruitment firm Randstad, over a 3 year period, showed that British workers were amongst the least satisfied in Europe.

There is such a body of evidence here, and I have only shared some of it with you. I could go on emphasising the point further, but I think I have made my point to you as the reader. This should be a call to arms.............. for all leaders in UK organisations.............. to 'pull up our socks' and do something about business culture.

What are you doing about your own business culture...............and the engagement of your people? Is there a long term plan to get better engagement of your people? It directly affects the performance of your business. If we know that is true..................we should have a programme to drive up engagement; to enhance our culture.............and to inspire our people. The

prize is more discretionary effort.......better customer service.................more innovations and ideas.........
......and ultimately outperformance of our competitors!

The best CEOs already 'get' the fact that their role is to create the right culture................in which their people can perform. As a leader............this has to become a big part of your role. If you are stuck in the day to day, and ignoring the bigger cultural picture...............the implication is that you will underperform. The potential of your people and the business performance will also suffer as a result.

CHAPTER 4

Talking To CEOs About
Culture And Performance

"Turned on people figure out how to beat the competition. Turned off people only complain about being beaten by the competition" Ben Simonton

"When people go to work, they shouldn't have to leave their hearts at home" Betty Bender

"Employees engage with employers and brands when they're treated as humans worthy of respect" Meghan Biro

WHAT CEOs SAY ABOUT THEIR CULTURE AND THEIR PERFORMANCE

I now spend much of my working time speaking to business conferences; to CEO Forums and to Boards in companies about the subjects of culture/engagement and high performance...............I also have the privilege of mentoring CEOs and other executives. In this context, I regularly discuss with CEOs their views on culture, engagement and the link between their people and the performance of their respective businesses.

Many of these CEOs have lived through testing times, either because of external recessionary pressures; or turbulence in their own industry sector; or sometimes inheriting an internally created crisis from a past leader. Other CEOs are in the polar opposite situation, with strong growth, and have to wrestle with the challenges of coping with expansion, including the need for capital and finding/hiring new talent.

Whatever the context, those CEOs are looking for ways to improve their culture; the morale of their teams; and to motivate their people to high levels of performance. They all readily articulate their view that the effect of culture on performance is 'massive'.

I will try to reflect in this book, the enthusiasm I have personally encountered, from CEOs who are keen to develop and maintain a high performance culture with a highly engaged and innovative workforce. The level of interest that I have encountered amongst 'switched on' CEOs for the topic of developing a healthy culture through engaging people is growing all the time. More and more 'enlightened' business leaders just 'get it', and are keen for tips and tools to enhance their culture, and make their enterprise a great place to work.

The rise in the number of organisations wanting to participate in UK national surveys, such as the Sunday Times 'Great Places to Work', is an indicator of this trend, and the thirst for progress on this agenda. It is a general observation, that when a subject such as culture and engagement becomes a 'hot topic' amongst top notch CEOs, then this becomes a very real crucible for innovation and progress in high performing cultures. I will be sharing some of the thoughts of these progressive CEOs as the book unfolds.

CULTURE DEFINITELY TRUMPS STRATEGY – THAT'S THE CEO VIEW

CEOs of yesteryear used to be focused purely on the P&L; the strategy and their stakeholders. Today, CEOs are increasingly aware that culture trumps strategy, and that unless they have a people and culture agenda – their results will not be maximized. Great CEOs are aware that their business can be seriously blown off course by the effects of a poor culture...............initiated by a lack of engagement with their people. It is possible to have a game changing strategy, but to fail because people are not with you.

Great CEOs know that a major part of their role is to keep their workforce motivated, superbly well informed...........and thereby create a loyal employee base. They have realised that attracting great new talent will only occur if the organisation is reputed externally to have a great culture. If your cultural reputation is poor the extremely savvy top talent won't come to work for you. Great people have a list of companies they want to work for, and that is principally down to the kind of culture and values they want to align with.

Keeping your people happy, in the performance zone, and giving willingly of their discretionary effort because they believe in the mission and the leadership ....is the objective of those top CEOs I have met and spoken with. They also know this is not a one off task! This has to become a way of life. Strong culture is not a destination...................it is a continuous journey. If you're not building your culture, it will automatically decline. Your culture is only as good as your current leadership input to it. This subject is something great leadership teams are always working on. Even the best cultures, having experienced a period of inferior leadership...............will inevitably begin to decay.

As I write and you read.....................I wonder if you are one of those 'switched on' CEOs or leaders? Or do you regard the whole debate on culture/engagement and the link to performance as a popular fad? I suppose the fact you are reading this book means that you have more than a passing interest in the causal links to gain high performance. I will try to give you some stories that will inspire you to pursue the building of a high performance culture in your own organisation.

Personally, I have read an awful lot of articles and material about 'the usual suspects' in terms of culture. The great exemplars quoted tend to be the Googles and the Apples of this world. Many people aspire to work for these companies. Yes I have been to the Google offices and seen the free fruit bowls and the creative thinking spaces. However, I think it worthwhile to write about companies and organisations which are less well known. I have chatted with a large number of CEOs over the past 8 years, and I want to share some thoughts about strong cultures which are certainly less well publicised than the global giants of the technology world.

This is not a research text, and nor is it an academic book. My observations are not some scientific theory. I offer you the observations of a lifetime practitioner. I am someone who talks to real people in the business world about the challenges of running real businesses. I keenly listen and observe and 'feel' real cultures and take in the difference in performance data. I am very much drawn to simplicity and things which are practical for operators in the real world.

Complexity kills initiatives. If I come up with some complex agenda, then you are unlikely to enact it. Most people running businesses and teams are looking for simple solutions, things which are actionable for the busy leader. Real people are inspired by real stories they can relate to.

YOU CAN 'FEEL' A CULTURE AS YOU ENTER THE PREMISES

My regular observation (and I go into many different types and sizes of business) is that you can 'feel' the culture. It's almost the smell of the place. When I am consulting; or speaking; or mentoring executives – entering the premises gives you an immediate impression of the place. The way people greet you, the reception experience, the speed at which people walk all tell you a lot about the culture of a workplace. New employees commencing get that same 'feel' as they commence their work.

Culture is something you 'feel' as an individual. Engagement is not something a company 'does' to the workforce. Peter Cheese, CEO of the CIPD believes that employees today expect a degree of personalisation at work, and for their individual opinions to be heard by the business. We have moved from the era of collectivism (where employees were a homogenous whole) to the era of the individual. Individuals have always mattered, except today they matter even more because they have vastly increased personal expectations of the place they go to work in.

We probably all know the John Lewis employment model – from the perspective of employing 'partners' who have an ownership stake in the business. What is less well known about John Lewis, is that they have openly acknowledged that engaging their people in a real and substantial way costs them money. John Lewis shows the cost of engagement on their balance sheet – counterbalanced by the benefits reaped in productivity. That seems to me to be the most overt acknowledgement of the cost of cultural progress and the benefits being represented in a company P&L.

CULTURE: IT'S A LINE RESPONSIBILITY

My firm view is that the driving of the link between culture and performance is certainly not the role of the 'HR function' – or whatever you call it in your business. Cultural activity is a line management function. Having a cultural progress agenda is a strategic imperative – and the CEO should be driving it through the line.

CHAPTER 5

Are The Principles Of Building A High Performance Culture At Asda Applicable Elsewhere?

"We have a culture where we are incredibly self-critical, we don't get comfortable with our success" Mike Parker – CEO Nike

"Corporate culture is the only sustainable competitive advantage that is completely within the control of the entrepreneur" David Cummings, Pardot

"As we look ahead into the 21st century, leaders will be those who empower others" Bill Gates

LEARNING TAKEN FROM THE ASDA CULTURAL/ PERFORMANCE TURNAROUND

My 15 years at Asda Stores – 10 years of which were as a member of the Executive Board, provided me with the perfect case study for major cultural change. The Asda business came perilously close to bankruptcy in the early 1990s, and that burning platform of a really serious business crisis afforded the opportunity to engineer major change to so many things in the business which were broken and malfunctioning. When you take a broken culture in a large and geographically spread business, and seek to re-engage a disillusioned workforce, you inevitably learn a lot of valuable lessons about what works and what does not work – on a practical basis.

My first book 'Asda Magic – the 7 principles of building a high performance culture', charts the most influential elements of changing a culture from disaster to world class excellence and high performance – over a 15 year timescale.

Doing things which subsequently produced great engagement of people, and built a high performance culture, certainly made a significant difference to the performance at Asda. The culture brought the strategy to life, and was material to Asda becoming Britain's No1 Best Place to Work in the Sunday Times survey of 2002. Not only that, it also contributed to the huge commercial turnaround from near bankruptcy to financial and sales outperformance in a highly competitive market – the UK food sector being probably the most competitive retail market in the world.

ARE THESE 7 PRINCIPLES TRANSFERRABLE TO OTHER BUSINESSES?

The question in your mind is – can I use these 7 principles to effect performance in my business? I set out over the past 8 years, to spot other businesses where the CEO was using the same principles to develop a positive culture of high performance.

In very simple terms....................my answer would be yes. I see elements of the Asda 7 principles case study in so many organisations. Maybe not with exactly the same emphasis, because each business is better at some cultural elements than others – but generally – the 7 principles appear in great cultures I have experienced on a regular basis. I will share some of those stories with you in subsequent chapters of this book.

Before sharing those stories, I would like to discuss the correlation of my 7 principles with so many other 'authorities' in this same area of knowledge.

ENGAGE FOR SUCCESS – DAVID McLEOD

The McLeod Review, which founded the 'Engage for Success' movement, found 4 main drivers of organizational success:-

i. A clear & compelling strategic narrative of the organisation's purpose/values and direction – employees need to be inspired (this equates to my own principle Communicate/communicate/communicate – to be engaged in a culture, people need to be inspired by what they hear from leaders).

ii. There have to be genuine opportunities for 'employee voice' to be heard and acted upon daily. Line Manager listening & responding is important (this is firmly in line with my own principle of systematic regular listening to people, and being seen to respond – even if the answer is negative).

iii. Good management & leadership behaviours need to make employees feel respected (my own principle here is choosing an appropriate modern style of leadership).

iv. Finally, Engage for Success speaks about the importance of organisational integrity, where people behave in ways which engender trust. (for me – I believe trust emerges from the combination of inspiring and truthful communication taking place regularly and consistently – together with responsive listening to employee voice – and brought together by a modern style of leadership - where managers truly 'walk the talk').

DAN PINK – IN HIS BOOK 'DRIVE'

Dan Pink, in his book 'Drive' talks about the power of performance coming from 3 principal things:-

i. Autonomy : organisations giving the individual more autonomy in the making of decisions.
ii. Mastery : making your employees feel recognised in the fact that they are making a contribution (this is one of my 7 principles – making great use of recognition is a powerful force in engaging people within a culture).
iii. Purpose : this is something more than profit or self-interest. People need to know they are doing something worthwhile. (This equates back to the David McLeod purpose and values and my communication principle).

KEVIN CRUSE : ENGAGEMENT IN A SENTENCE

Kevin's formula for high engagement and a strong culture is that "people give loyalty and discretionary effort to those who foster growth, show appreciation, share a compelling vision and are trustworthy".

In Kevin's sentence are encapsulated several of my 7 principles; A great style of leadership; inspiring and trustworthy communication and showing appreciation/ recognition. I think we are seeing common threads here in what many people are saying about culture and engagement.

WHAT ABOUT FUN AT WORK?

Interestingly, neither McLeod nor Pink talk about having fun at work. Yet it is one of my 7 principles. Henry Stewart certainly majors on fun in his book 'The Happy Manifesto'. His own training company Happy Ltd has featured strongly in the Sunday Times Best Places to Work survey over many years.

Gant, the U.S. clothing business have consistently featured in the U.S. Best Place to work survey (equivalent to the Sunday Times survey in the UK). Gant firmly believes work and play should co-exist. They think it's a well-kept secret, and yet a fun place to work makes you attractive to recruits of a high calibre and potential high performance.

There are various studies out there which back up the fact that having fun in your workplace increases productivity and creativity – leads to real pride in the business and also breeds loyalty at high levels. When people are having fun, and collaborate together, they feel like they are on the same team and pulling together. That camaraderie and banter builds trust in the teams and vicariously in the business. I experienced the power of fun in the Asda culture, and consequently have it as one of my principles. I believe it matters, and so do the 'switched on' CEOs that I meet.

FINDING EXEMPLARS OF THE 7 PRINCIPLES

Having shown you the close thinking about what makes up strong cultures and engagement of people to produce high performance – I am now going to move on to exemplars of my 7 principles in subsequent chapters.

CHAPTER 6

Hiring For Attitude – Training For Skill

WHO YOU HIRE HAS ALWAYS BEEN HUGELY IMPORTANT TO CULTURE

"Create the kind of workplace and company culture that will attract great talent. If you hire brilliant people, they will make work feel like play" Richard Branson

"Pick out associates whose behaviour is better than yours and you'll drift in that direction" Warren Buffet

"You absolutely must have the discipline not to hire until you find the right people" Jim Collins

"We believe that it is really important to come up with core values that you can commit to, and by commit, we mean you're willing to hire and fire, based on them. If you're willing to do that, then you're well on the way to building a company culture that is in line with the brand you want to build" Tony Hsieh – CEO Zappos.com

"Shaping your culture is more than half done when you hire your team" Jessica Herrin – Stella & Dot

HIRING – THE BIGGEST CULTURAL SIGNAL YOU CAN POSSIBLY SEND

I often say to clients – the biggest signal you ever send to your own people about your culture is when you hire someone. That brand new shiny employee with no miles on their clock will either enhance or detract from the culture – from day 1.

In my experience, existing employees have a polarised reaction to new recruits. They either love them or hate them. This reaction rarely falls into the neutral zone.

Don't ever think that hiring just fills a gap. If you get this wrong, it will switch off the effort of many co-workers. Get it right, and people's confidence in you grows, and everyone lifts their efforts. Make sure you hire people that will fit your culture, and add to your direction of travel. Brilliant hires have a bigger effect than plus one. Bad hires have a bigger effect in the wrong direction than just one mistake.

HIRING – SO EASY TO GET WRONG

Recruiting great people is extremely hard. Even executives with decades of experience in hiring will readily tell you they only call it right 75% of the time.

If hiring is easy to get wrong, and you will inevitably make hiring mistakes, then the effect on your organisation's culture is massive.................so you need to move quickly if you make a mistake. Hiring either 'lifts' everyone because the hire is good, or is a 'downer' for everyone's performance. This is not something where you can afford to sit on the fence. People resent under-performers, and misfits to the culture will cause total effort to decline. Great people, by contrast, add more than the sum of their ability to total effort, because the converse is also true. People love great hires, and it causes morale to rise, and effort to expand dis-proportionately.

We tend to hold back on removing wrong hires because of two things. Firstly, our own ego gets in the way. We have to admit, to ourselves and others that we have made a mistake, and so we tend to defend the position. Secondly, we also feel it is fair to give people opportu-nity to improve. We have just hired them from previous employment, in most cases, and we feel obligated to give them a chance. The workforce, however, will be much more desperate for us to remove wrong hires, and until we do, it will affect the effort of all.

ZAPPOS – PAY MISTAKEN HIRES TO GO

Tony Hsieh, the CEO of Zappos.com (an online shoe retailer – now part of Amazon), learnt the hard way about hiring for attitude. He began to realise that culture was the number one element for success, and that hiring was a vital part of developing a culture. Tony admits that Zappos didn't know what they were doing with hiring during the start up of the company. Tony thought a great C.V. and great experience must be good. He quickly realised that screening for a candi-date's alignment with the Zappos company values mattered much more. Zappos began to listen to their 'gut' experience when hiring – looking especially at how candidate attitudes were presented to them.

Tony utilized the views of the shuttle driver who drove candidates from the airport for interview. He realised that if executives treat the 'little' people badly, he should not hire them, no matter how technically capable they might be. Tony also asked executives to go and take calls in the Zappos call centre for the first 2 weeks, before commencing their role. If that didn't go well, Zappos wouldn't hire them. These are good 'rules of thumb' in the hiring process. Ask around for views on candidates, and give them actual basic work to do, to see what they are really like as people.

Zappos also offer to pay people $3000/4000 at the end of their first week to leave, if they want to do so. They don't want people who don't fit to feel trapped. As a consequence of this policy, 2/3% of their new hires have historically taken the money and gone. A really healthy practice.

Tony Hsieh of Zappos embodies many of the beliefs on hiring, which I consider to be a vital necessity in building a high performance culture. Hiring for attitude; using your gut on who you hire; assessing candidates using more than interviewing, and removing quickly any mistakes you make where people don't fit your culture.

ICELAND - RECRUITING HAPPY PEOPLE WITH THE RIGHT ATTITUDES

Malcolm Walker is a colourful character of a CEO, at the Frozen Food retailer Iceland. He featured in a BBC2 series entitled 'Life in the freezer', where he extolled the virtue of recruiting happy people. Malcolm's view, which I totally share, was that you cannot teach great customer service to the wrong people. You have to hire the kind of enthusiastic & motivated people, to whom you can then give the necessary service skills. The raw material of the right kind of personality matters.

Iceland is the only company I know, other than my own time at Asda, which employs assessment centre techniques to shop floor hiring. Iceland clearly hires for attitude, and I'm sure that this strategy was instrumental in their achieving No1 Best Place to work in the Sunday Times 2012 survey, and No2 position in the same survey in 2013. Who you hire matters massively to your culture and performance.

JOHN LEWIS – BIG ON ATTITUDE & BEHAVIOURS IN HIRING

Another household name where they believe in hiring for attitude and behaviour is the John Lewis partnership. JLP have identified a set of behaviours upon which to base their selection. They major on building trust in leaders and also in those being led, and therefore the right kind of attitudes and behaviours are crucial. JLP are not explicit about every detail of behaviour, they just want recruits who instinctively 'get' what they are trying to do. People with the right attitude when hired, will fit their culture and behave in the right way.

PRÉT A MANGER – OBSESSIVE ABOUT HIRING THE RIGHT 'FIT'

Prét is another company who are obsessive about hiring to 'fit' the culture. Before anyone joins their central operations, they have to spend a week in store serving food and drinks to customers, in order to learn all about how the front line works. Those front line team members are consulted about those potential hires – to assess whether they are made of the 'right stuff'.

Apparently a potential Chief Financial Officer had his offer rescinded because the in store team felt he wasn't a Prét person. This type of behaviour is very powerful. It recognises how important culture is to the future success of the business.

TIMPSON – RECRUIT NICE PEOPLE AND TRUST THEM

A UK business I greatly admire is Timpson, the shoe repair and key cutting business (with over 800 outlets around the country) run by CEO James Timpson. James told me that their philosophy is to hire 'nice people', and then trust them to make the right decisions. James thinks that most textbooks on the subject of customer service are 'complete rubbish'. He feels that they give too little emphasis to the importance of the hiring decision. James says that Timpson are very 'black or white' on what they think about people. They either like you, or they want you to leave.

Their broad mindedness as to where the 'right attitude' might come from extends to the hiring of a lot of ex-offenders. They also ask candidates to spend a day working in one of their branches, in order to get an experienced hand to assess whether they will 'fit' the culture. They deploy a mandatory trial period of 16 weeks before they finally say yes to any new hire. Timpson, as an organisation, realise the importance of the decision about who you hire. They view hiring for skill as lazy recruitment, and in my view.................if you hire for skill alone, it will inevitably go wrong.

AO.COM – IT'S ALL ABOUT ATTITUDE

When interviewing John Roberts, the CEO of DRL, parent company of online appliances retailer AO.com, he explained that for him hiring was all about attitude. Despite a difficult float in 2014, this is a remarkable business, which was founded in 2000 after a £1 bet between John Roberts and a mate, that he could simplify the supply chain for white goods, and deliver using the internet.

John Roberts looks to get the best people by measuring their 'DNA' as he calls it. The business looks for attitudes and characteristics in people concerning fun; trust; humility; resilience; positivity; passion and adaptability.

AO.com doesn't for instance recruit delivery drivers, it recruits people who have the right attitude to give great customer service...............who can also drive a delivery vehicle. They have a strong similarity with Zappos. com, in that...............if induction isn't working for you, you can immediately take a month's pay to leave. They have only ever had a few entrants do this, but it is a great safety valve for mistakes. If AO.com finds you don't fit, they will remove you. They really know how important to their culture this is.

HOW MANY EXEMPLARS DO YOU NEED TO PROVE THE POINT?

Hiring for attitude is critical to switched on businesses. I could tell you about Innocent Drinks, who decoded their values and recruited against them. They realised that their culture was everything in a high growth business.

L.V. Insurance have spent a number of years successfully hiring for attitude in another very successful business.

I could go on quoting exemplars, but I think the point I have been hammering home in this chapter, is that hiring for attitude works. Successful and savvy CEOs, running fast moving successful businesses, believe that hiring the right people will produce performance results which will astound you. They know that hiring executives who fit your culture, means that they will naturally take the organisation to a better place, whereas the converse is also true, that bad fit hires will take you in the wrong direction.

HIRING – THE No1 INDICATOR OF CULTURE

My own experience tells me that the hiring decision is the number one flag to existing employees about the health of your culture and where it is heading. If you get your hiring right, it has an immediate and positive effect on everyone's performance. Do not underestimate the power of this principle.................or it will cost you dearly as an organisation. I'm totally with those CEOs who believe that shaping your culture is more than half done when you hire your team.

SUMMARY POINTS:

- Give most weight to 'fit'
- Take time to hire right
- Consult employees
- Get candidates to do some real work for you
- Realise interviews alone will produce defective hiring decisions

YOUR ACTIONS:

Make sure you get behind the mask to see the real person

What will you change about your hiring process?

CHAPTER 7

Communicate, Communicate, Communicate

COMMUNICATIONS : THE 'ROCKET FUEL' OF A HIGH PERFORMANCE CULTURE

"The single biggest problem in communication is the illusion that it has taken place" George Bernard Shaw

"It's not all about content. It's all about stories.................great stories" Mitch Joel

"Information is giving out, communication is getting through" Sydney J Harris

"Communication is a skill you can learn. If you are willing to work at it, you can rapidly improve the quality of every part of your life" Brian Tracy

"Good communication is as stimulating as black coffee, and just as hard to sleep after" Anne Morrow Lindbergh

KEEPING YOUR PEOPLE 'IN THE LOOP' REALLY MAKES A DIFFERENCE TO PERFORMANCE

It's a horrible experience when something happens in your own workplace, which you knew nothing about beforehand. You're 'out of the loop', and it makes you feel demoralised and demotivated. I'm sure we've all experienced this phenomenon at some early stage in our careers...............when someone deemed that we were not senior enough to be 'in the know'.

Conversely, if you have been well briefed and this happens regularly, the feeling of being 'in the loop' is very motivational. Regularity of communication means that you always know what is going on before things happen at your place of work...................and that builds the all-important commodity..............trust. You begin to have the feeling that 'this is my business', and you will automatically give more discretionary effort.

THE MORE PEOPLE KNOW THE MORE THEY WILL CARE

It is my firm belief, and experience, that the more people know in the workplace, the more they will care. This is a key factor in building a highly motivated and high performance workplace. It shouldn't be just the senior team or just the Board of an organisation who are 'in the know'.

Great communication is the rocket fuel of a high performance culture, and we need to realise just how vital it is to keep people superbly well informed.

CEOs KNOW COMMUNICATION MATTERS –
WORKERS SAY THEY ARE ALWAYS IN THE DARK!!

Every CEO I talk to, or work with, seems to emphasise the importance of communicating with their workforce. They talk to me about the effort they are putting into getting their strategic plans known and understood...........and also making sure people can keep track of the 'scores on the doors'.

Yet whenever I go into client businesses to listen to their workforce, they always say that no one tells them anything. I find this a fascinating phenomenon. I'm convinced those CEOs are not lying to me about their intention to ensure communication happens. I'm also convinced the employees are quite serious when they say "we're in the dark".

INFORMATION OVERLOAD IN
PRESENT DAY SOCIETY

My analysis of the communication issue, is that in-company communication is falling foul of what is happening to humans in modern society. Employees are not separate from the world in which we all live. Employees are being bombarded with information almost every waking moment. We know what is happening worldwide..........with 24 hour rolling news............we have social media hitting phones during the day.............and we have business communication overload in the form of the dreaded email. We have music streamed to our phones so people can listen if there is a gap in other activity. No wonder we don't hear those important communications in the workplace..............they are lost like a 'needle in a haystack'.

If that important briefing was sent via email, it will be lost in a forest of other email traffic. If your prime communication tool is email, you may as well not have bothered.

REPETITION IS THE 'MOTHER OF LEARNING' – YOU HAVE TO REPEAT MESSAGES TO GET THROUGH

Employees today have busy minds which are receiving information from multiple sources all the time. We have to break through that 'noise' of modern life as leaders who want to communicate effectively. My mantra on this is communicate, communicate, communicate. If you re-emphasise and repeat key messages, then you are more likely to penetrate that noisy modern life people are living.

The unfortunate truth, for executives then, is that the only way to become a world class communicator with your own people, is to become doggedly repetitive. Communicate, communicate and communicate some more if you really want to break through. When your people comment that you seem to 'keep banging on' about a particular theme, then you know you are getting through the 'static noise' barrier.

The problem is that executives don't enjoy having to repeat themselves. It's boring! The paradigm in executive thinking says "I'm the boss, they should listen to me...............I shouldn't have to repeat myself."

My message to all who are in leadership in any organisation or team, is that no matter what your pay grade or level of importance (and that includes the CEO) you do need to repeat yourself, or what you say will be lost in the noise of modern life.

FACE TO FACE COMMUNICATION BEATS ALL OTHER MEANS

Some CEOs tell me, in all sincerity, that they communicate regularly with their employees using email updates. They think that gets the job done. It's easy for them to do................and they justify it by telling me that their people are geographically dispersed.

Now, I do believe that email was a wonderful innovation.............especially for short quick updates. That ability to know you have got an important one liner to someone's hand held device is the basis of Twitter and Snapchat and the like.

But, the effectiveness of email in business was quickly 'mired' by huge over use. The problem now, is that people often receive hundreds of emails each day. They have transitioned from time saver to time thief.

I still believe that seeking to inspire individuals face to face is what makes the difference in being a world class communicator. Any written form of communication, whether by email or whatever, is often misunderstood...............not completely read, and quickly lost in the morass of more information.

By speaking with people, you can gauge reaction, understanding, and the likelihood of good implementation. That's real communication.

CAFFE NERO – THE CEO NEEDS TO COMMUNICATE THE VISION

Caffe Nero, the high street coffee chain, has been managing double digit sales growth over an extended period of time..........whilst managing the stresses and strains of huge business expansion over a lengthy period. Their view as a business, is that at least 50% of customers make repeat visits for coffee, because they form relationships with Nero employees. In other words, it's at least as much about human relationships as it is about coffee.

Nero believe it is the CEOs job to focus on effective communication of the vision, whilst seeking feedback from employees. They are not alone..................my belief is that success and growth are always founded on great effective and regular communication from the top.

ADMIRAL INSURANCE – COMMUNICATION BUILDS TRUST; ENGAGEMENT AND PRIDE

In 2013, Admiral Insurance came 2nd in the Sunday Times Great Places to work list for large companies in the UK, and also for European employers. Admiral is an organisation which believes in the excellence of communicating strategy and direction of the company to its people. They regularly communicate how they are doing and also where they want to get to. Communication is one of Admiral's strongest processes, and they have sought to use both formal and informal methods, to ensure communication cascades from the Boardroom to all their employees.

All the high performing companies, who have done well in the Great Places to work surveys, are those who work really hard at building trust through effective internal communications.

RSA – COMMUNICATION EFFECTIVENESS IS LINKED TO DISCRETIONARY EFFORT

Another insurance company that believes in regular effective communication with all employees is RSA (previously known as Royal Sun Alliance). The CEO, who came in to reorganize the business, emphasised the importance of internal communication, by introducing a process called 'up close and personal'. Employees were briefed in groups of 20/30 on a regular basis, about what was going on in the organisation.

RSA defined capable leaders as those who were able to focus on honest and transparent communication with their people. I particularly like that definition. It is both simple and effective. People can only ever do the right things in the right way, if they know exactly what is expected of them. They also need regular feedback on how they are doing. What is going well, and what is not going well. Regular communication is vital to creating a high performance culture.

RSA claims to be the world's most engaged insurance company. It came 6th in the Sunday Times 25 Best Big

Companies to work for in 2012, and won People Management Magazine's overall employer award from the CIPD in 2012. RSA has moved from a low morale business, with disappointing financial returns, to feeling able to claim its place as the world's most engaged insurer. The key to their turnaround, was leaders who communicated and built the trust of a workforce of 23,000 people.

WHITBREAD – WALKING ABOUT & TALKING TO PEOPLE

Many CEOs will tell you that the City is not really interested in culture, just financial results. Whitbread is a business which has had some very robust debates around the importance of culture, around its Board table.

The acquisition of Premier Lodge, for £0.5billion, involved 2 months of Board members visiting sites, and just walking around talking to the people on site. The objective was to get the people on board with the plans for the business by communicating informally with them. Whitbread say that the integration of the acquisition into their business went much quicker and smoother than expected...............because of that investment of time taken just talking informally with people. Investment in communication is always time which yields results.

It stands to reason for me................the more people know......the more they will care. The better informed your people are, the more motivated and effective they become.

UNIPART – COMMUNICATION THROUGH
THE HARD TIMES

Great communication isn't just for the good times, or for major organisational change.................it is even more vital in the tough times. Building trust, by regularly keeping people 'in the loop' is extremely motivational..............but it also builds a reserve of trust...... which can be called upon in the tough times.

Unipart experienced this in the 2009 automotive recession, which hit suppliers like Unipart very hard. Unipart found that regularly briefing people meant that engagement actually increased during the recessionary period. Employees understood the situation of the business very clearly, and believed they were being treated fairly during tough times.................this was clearly based on the trust built up in leadership through good communication, over time.

Unipart used 'communication cells', providing a framework for daily team briefings, and giving teams problem solving tools to work on emerging issues. Communication that is honest in crisis can build morale and productivity against external threats................and this was the experience at Unipart through the recession.

NEVER UNDERESTIMATE THE POWER OF
EFFECTIVE REGULAR COMMUNICATION

Genuine, trustworthy communication, repeated regularly..............is one of the cornerstones of a healthy high performance culture. Where people feel they can be open and honest, involvement is stimulated, and people are far more likely to give of their discretionary effort.

True performance cultures are founded on regular, reliable and inspirational communication. This is a long term philosophy. Being a great communicator requires determination to do it...........week in.....week out...............without fail. Do it well, and it will become the 'rocket fuel' of a high performance culture.

SUMMARY POINTS:

- Do you have a way of cascading information about strategy & performance on a regular basis?
- Are you a great storyteller – and do you encourage others to tell stories to embed messages?
- Is there too much email in your business and not enough face to face?
- Do you constantly repeat key messages?
- What level of trust have you built up in your organisation?
- Do you tell people as much as possible as early as possible?

YOUR ACTIONS:

What will you do to revolutionise communication in you organisation?

Are you serious about becoming a world class communicator?

CHAPTER 8

Listening

BEING A GREAT LISTENER IS A POWERFUL DRIVER OF A PERFORMANCE CULTURE

"Listen more & talk less. Take notes...........lots of notes. If you don't write down spontaneous ideas, they can be gone in the blink of an eye. You'll be amazed at the challenges a listening culture can overcome." Richard Branson

"A hallmark of a healthy creative culture is that people feel free to share ideas, opinions and criticisms. Lack of candour, if unchecked, leads to dysfunctional environments." Ed Catmull, Pixar

"The role of a great leader is not to have all the ideas; it's to create a culture where everyone can have ideas and feel they're valued." Ken Robinson

"When you give everyone a voice & give people power, the system usually ends up in a really good place." Mark Zuckerberg

"An effective leader is also an effective listener."
Artika Tyner

"I learned to listen by having only one objective:
comprehension. I was only trying to understand
what the person was trying to convey to me. I
wasn't listening to critique; to object or to con-
vince. I was listening solely to comprehend." Sam
Palmisano CEO IBM

I'M A DELIBERATE ACTIVE LISTENER

People often tell me I have a defining characteristic...
...........I am a good listener. It is a skill I have sought to
cultivate in business life. I realised early in my career,
how important it was to understand where others were
coming from.

I have also worked with so many people who were ego
obsessive, and rarely, if ever, asked what others were
thinking. A major failing for a rounded top class executive is to be a poor listener.

RICHARD BRANSON – GOOD LISTENING MAY BE A 'DYING ART'

Richard Branson devotes 25% of his book 'the Virgin
way', to the subject of listening. He states that listening
is a dying art. I find therefore, that I have a great deal in
common with him as a leader. Ever since my schooldays
– being taught by a history master by the name of Bill

Walker – I learned to take excellent notes of what I was being taught. Not only did I take great notes at school, I carried that through to college, and so into the workplace. I learned to take great action notes in meetings – I perfected the art of fast legible handwriting for examinations............and never lost it. My day books at work became a record of my daily working life, and enabled me never to forget an action or an idea.

Richard Branson, it turns out, is exactly the same, but for different reasons. Being dyslexic, Richard listened to people very carefully, and wrote notes of everything he was told in hardback notebooks – and says that they served him incredibly well in major lawsuits with the likes of British Airways and T Mobile. He could quote verbatim what people had said in meetings, because he had the notes.

Richard says, quite correctly in my view, that listening is a wonderful and much under-rated skill. The brain remembers such a small percentage of what we hear – and writing in notebooks recalls so much valuable information, which can then be referred back to at a later date. He is singularly unimpressed with executives who don't take notes. His contention is "how on earth can you retain even 10% of what is being said in day long meetings without taking copious notes?" I totally agree with him. Richard cites the example of Sir Stelios Ioannou – the founder of Easyjet – as another great listener and note taker.

The Richard Branson mantra on this topic is to become known as a great listener if you want to become a great leader. He also recommends listening for what is not said, as well as what is said. A great tip!

EMPATHETIC ACTIVE LISTENING

Leaders who can suspend their own frame of reference to listen actively/empathetically to the other person, have a great gift. Listening in this way is so often at odds with today's fast moving; multi- tasking; information overloaded; distraction driven world. Leaders who listen at all, are often waiting for the other person to stop, so that they can speak. That's not listening. Real listening is so important.

Being able to regularly and systematically listen to the thoughts, views and ideas of the people who work for you, is a key tool in the armoury of a high performance culture. The highest form of respect you can pay to an individual is to listen to them.

LISTENING – ONE OF STEPHEN COVEY'S 7 HABITS

Stephen Covey's 7 Habits of highly effective people, includes this ability to use empathetic listening – he terms this 'seek first to understand' (that means suspending judgement and listening to points of view other than your own).

Covey's 7 Habits

1. Be proactive
2. Begin with the end in mind
3. Put first things first
4. Think 'win-win'

5. Seek first to understand (be a great listener)
6. Synergise
7. 'Sharpen the saw'

Covey believes we are moving from the industrial age, where leaders had formal authority, to the age of the knowledge worker, and moral authority............. people have to have trust between each other and open dialogue.............which taps into the creative energies and ideas of people to improve the performance of the business.

Covey thinks businesses should involve their people in decision making, to work out solutions together. He believes better solutions will always be reached by empathetic listening to others.

This very much plays to the belief that none of us is as smart as all of us. Consequently, leaders who systematically listen to the views, ideas and thoughts of people within the organisation, will always tap into a rich seam of thought and often key solutions to emerging issues.

What evidence have I gathered of great listening by exemplar organisations? The first case study I wish to use is that of Pets at Home.

PETS AT HOME – COLLEAGUES HAVE REAL 'CLOUT'

Pets at Home is another retail business which has done particularly well in the Sunday Times index of Best Places to work in the U.K. Internally, Pets' own survey of morale sits around the 90% satisfaction mark, and the business has a net promoter score of 84%.

Pets has had an infusion of executives with Asda 'DNA', so it is little surprise to me that the business has made strong progress with both its culture and performance. The two things go 'hand in hand'.

Pets believe in putting the customer at the heart of their business, using regular systematic colleague and customer listening groups. They use some traditional research data, but colleague views have real 'clout', because they know directly what customers are saying they want from the business. Colleagues in the front line are interacting with customers on a daily basis, and so are the best authority on what customers are saying. The business gives fast informal response to colleague feedback – since it realises the power of listening to its people.

This is not 'rocket science', but it is extremely powerful when done well – and is clearly a huge attribute to the Pets business.

AO.COM – LISTENING TO THE RIVER – 'DRIVER POWER'

I have already cited the example of the strong performance culture at AO.com, via their 'hiring for attitude' strategy. Here again, I am giving them credit for great listening mechanics. John Roberts, their charismatic CEO meets all his delivery drivers around every 6 to 9 months. He talks to them about what's happening in the business (sending messages), but the real purpose of those sessions is to leave them the space to say whatever they wish to say (regular systematic listening). This mechanism leaves the CEO to decide on the matters they raise – and sometimes he can do it there and then (if appropriate). John told me the story of delivery drivers asking to wear shorts in the hot weather. This was a widely held view – raised by many of the drivers as he listened. He agreed there and then in his listening meetings, and was able to confirm the decision to the whole organisation within the week. The power of those symbolic 'moments' cannot be underestimated – they are motivational dynamite.

Sometimes John Roberts says no to comments made, but where he agrees to respond to an issue, he writes to all the delivery drivers in the business at their home address. This is a really important principle in my view – listening doesn't mean you always have to say yes – you should always listen with a discerning ear. When you do respond – it is important that everyone knows where the idea or suggestion came from – because that generates more ideas and solutions to issues. Writing to employees at home ensures that nothing falls through organisational cracks – and all drivers know what was agreed.

Employees treated in this way tend to care more about the business, because they can see their CEO responding. The effect on morale is electrifying. In my own experience, even saying "no" to certain ideas (because it was too expensive/or it wouldn't work) still has a net positive effect on morale if you explain the reasons for your decision. People will say that they feel better anyway because they have been allowed to 'get it off their chest'.

AMICUS HORIZON HOUSING ASSOCIATION – LISTENING IN ORDER TO TURN AROUND COMPLAINTS PROBLEMS

Amicus Housing Association was in a very bad place, with poor customer satisfaction, resulting from poor performance. The organisation was very unhappy with an underperforming culture. They state that the key to turnaround in their performance as a housing association, was in systematic listening. They listened to both their own people, and also their customers – the residents.

The organisation pursued a cultural turnaround, which encouraged senior leaders to listen to their people. When they began to get views back about how the association could do a better job, the most crucial response was to actually listen – rather than deny or defend. Leaders realised it was no good having a CEO sitting in an 'ivory tower'. Their view was, if you have a performance problem – you have got to take time to listen.

Their change of strategy, based upon systematic listening, created a climate of trust and respect................. and satisfaction with complaint handling improved from a very poor 55% to an excellent 95%. It is certainly true, that engaging managers are those who regularly listen, and use that listening to gather thoughts/ideas and solutions from their teams.

UNIPART – 'EMPLOYEE VOICE' IS A COMPETITIVE ADVANTAGE

I have already quoted Unipart as great believers in the power of regular communication with employees. They are also great exemplars of the power of employee listening. Their view is that listening to employees can provide competitive advantage.

Unipart believe that people working on the front line can often see opportunities that their managers would simply never know about. Faced with aggressive competition in their sector from China and India, the key to re-gaining competitive advantage (in their view) was in improving what they term 'employee voice'. Unipart takes the view that companies who do not utilise the power and potential of listening to 'employee voice' will inevitably be left behind.

This view would certainly correlate with survey results, showing that 75% of workers lose 2 working hours every week, because of unclear communication and feedback. I have often said that leadership sometimes gets in the way of productivity.........and causes inefficiency because leaders don't get sufficiently close to their people.

SALFORD NHS TRUST – 'LISTENING BY WALKING AROUND'

A great example of managers getting close to their people is the NHS Trust in Salford. This is an acute Trust, which has adopted a leadership style of listening to the front line. They decided to move from the more usual 'tell & sell' style, to deliberately listening to and coaching front line people. The Trust believed that front line workers had the best understanding of how to make beneficial changes to the operations. On infection control, for example, they talked directly to both nursing and clinical employees to elicit their views. They told them…. "If you agree with us that preventing infection is paramount, then we are open to ideas as to how to achieve that in your area."

Salford NHS Trust felt they should embrace the concept that employees be given the authority to find out what worked best, and feel supported in trying ideas out. If something didn't work, employees should not suffer detriment as a consequence……….but should feel free to try other solutions. Senior leaders deliberately engaged in 'walk arounds' to take ideas, and worked alongside front line teams, listening to their views.

Salford NHS Trust subsequently achieved the best employee engagement scores in England, in the national NHS morale survey. They put this significant achieve-ment down to the power of listening to their people………….and letting them find the best solution to problems.

It seems to me that many of the best solutions to issues in organisations come from the front line, rather than the Board room. Not all the best ideas in an organisa-tion are driven top down. Some of the best solutions are from the bottom up.

RESEARCH REVEALS A CHRONIC FAILURE TO LISTEN IN MANY ORGANISATIONS

There is no doubt that innovative ideas, give a business real 'edge' over competitors, but various research studies have revealed that employers are missing out on thousands of innovation opportunities each year ....because they don't listen to their people.

Research I have seen, shows that every employee, on average, has 6 innovative ideas to improve their business each year. Unfortunately, those employee ideas, which could potentially add real value to the bottom line, are lost because of the lack of any systematic listening process to collect and develop the ideas effectively. Worse still, 60% of employees could quote examples where suggestions for improvement to business processes have been actively ignored!

LISTENING IS A LEADERSHIP STRENGTH – NOT A SIGN OF WEAKNESS

Research by Stern & Duke Business Schools in the U.S. has shown that the more power leaders have, the less likely they are to take advice or listen to feedback. Powerful leaders tend to be confident, and this confidence has usually carried them to a position of seniority. Sadly, this also means they are just as confident when making sub-optimal or just plain wrong decisions!

The best leaders actually never abuse their positional power. They are happy to surround themselves with challenging people, and also to admit that they can never always be right. Great leaders realise............. that to get the best from the people they lead......they must connect.........listen and always value the input of others. My experience in this aspect tells me that this type of leader elicits better ideas and solutions, from a wide base of people, which in turn drives real improvement toward a high performing culture.

THE LAST WORD ON THE SUBJECT OF LISTENING GOES TO PROFESSOR JULIAN BIRKINSHAW OF LONDON BUSINESS SCHOOL

Julian Birkinshaw is a great lateral thinker. I have known him for some years, and he has insights about leading in the modern world which are quite radical. His view is that the speed of knowledge is so fast today, that it is very difficult for any of us individually to keep up!

Julian's view is that we have to become more agile, in order to cope with the speed of knowledge change, and the potential 'curved balls' which may come at us. A key tool, from his perspective, is listening to your people. Organisations need to be more capable of accessing the emotions and intuition of their people. Leaders in the past portrayed themselves as all knowing, and the conduits of handing down information to lesser mortals. Successful leaders of the future, in Julian's view, will be those who are best able to harness the emotions, convictions and thoughts of co-workers and customers in real time.

Are you a great listener? In order to compete in the world of today................you need to become one!!

SUMMARY POINTS:

- Do you have a systematic process for listening to your people and your customers?
- Could employees tell stories about ideas/innovations which have improved business performance?
- Do your people say "no one ever listens to us – we simply don't matter"?
- Do your employee's views have 'clout'?
- Do you see listening as a source of competitive advantage?
- Do you listen by walking around/rolling up your sleeves & working alongside the front line to elicit ideas?

YOUR ACTIONS:

What are you going to do to become a world class listener?

Do you keep a notebook of what people say?

CHAPTER 9

Choosing A Style Of Leadership

LEADERSHIP 'SETS A TONE' WHICH NEEDS TO WORK FOR THE MODERN WORLD

"Those who lead by example & demonstrate passion for what they do, make it easier for their followers to do the same." Coach Goldsmith

"Leadership consists of nothing but taking responsibility for everything that goes wrong, and giving your subordinates credit for everything that goes well." Dwight D. Eisenhower

"There are no good or bad Regiments. There are only good or bad officers." Field Marshall Bernard Montgomery (Monte)

"The price of leadership is to stay positive, whether you feel like it or not." Winston Churchill

"If your actions inspire others to dream more, do more & become more, you are a leader." John Quincy Adams

"Ultimately, it's on the company leaders to set the tone. If you select them so carefully that they in turn then hire the right people, it's a nice self-fulfilling prophecy." Tim Cook CEO Apple

"Always treat your people as you would want them to treat your best customers." Stephen R. Covey

WHAT STYLE OF LEADERSHIP WORKS IN THE WORLD OF TODAY?

I have a quote from Richard Branson concerning appropriate leadership style, which he believes creates the right culture for an organisation. Richard says "There is no magic formula for great company culture. The key is to treat your staff how you would like to be treated."

Now, I think Richard Branson has achieved much, and there is no doubt he is an innovator and a creative thinker. I have already cited his thinking with much admiration on the subject of listening. However, I personally deviate from this particular quote of his. Firstly, I do think there is some 'magic' in creating the right culture. Indeed, my first book was entitled 'Asda Magic – the 7 principles of building a high performance culture.' I believe it is possible to get this right, and enhance both culture and performance beyond what was naturally expected. I believe you can create some of this 'magic' for yourself, if you are prepared to work hard at the right agenda.

Secondly, I loathe the very word 'staff' used in Richard's quote. It grates on me. It is old fashioned terminology. It embodies an 'us and them' feeling. In a business you employ real people – not staff – because staff sounds subordinate. In the modern world – we should all want to be in this together. By all means use the terms 'our colleagues' or 'our people' – but never that demeaning phrase 'our staff'.

Thirdly, and most significantly, I believe great leaders should never say they treat people how they themselves would want to be treated. I know Richard is intending that to be a high standard................he wants to emphasise respecting others. However, I don't think you can ever achieve that by assuming everyone is like you. It is a form of generic leadership, which will be less effective than individual leadership. If you treat everyone the same, you will inevitably be loved be some and loathed by others. There is a tendency in generic leadership for those who think similarly to you to think you're great, but others who are unlike you will feel you don't really understand where they are coming from.

Leadership is about people. Leaders should take the time to find out what motivates and drives each individual. That knowledge enables you to manage them in such a way that they can thrive. My maxim would be to find out what makes each of your reports 'tick'. This takes time to do well, which is why so many leaders adopt a generic shorthand. Even Stephen Covey's quote of treating your people like you would treat your best customer is too generic for me to be comfortable with it. I believe that if you really learn about your people, you can manage each person individually. This enables you to treat them how they want to be treated. That way, you really will be pushing the boundaries, and accessing that 'magic' which is so evident in vibrant high performance cultures. We live in an individualistic world, and the younger employees are, the less forgiving they are of generic leadership styles.

LEADERS TEND TO THINK THEY'RE GREAT LEADERS – THEIR PEOPLE TEND TO DISAGREE

I find some CEOs can be far too flippant concerning their leadership style. They have told themselves that they are ok. That's the reason they have risen to 'running the show'.

In the 2015 'Britain at work' survey, a massive 92% of managers responded that they felt they had very good people skills. Sadly, employees do not agree. 32% think their manager doesn't communicate openly or honestly with them. 35% said that their manager did a lot of telling and not a lot of listening. 34% said they wanted more support from their manager. The killer statistic was that 49% (that's almost half of all the employees surveyed) said they would not recommend their organisation to new recruits. That's a leadership and cultural issue.

It doesn't sound to me as if 92% of leaders have good people skills from those survey statistics.........but there is a lot of self-delusion around.

Great leadership in the world of today, requires leaders to pay attention to the emotional climate of their team........deliberately creating an environment where they can thrive and achieve great results. Leaders need to be both visible and approachable. People need to feel they can come to you to discuss problems and issues freely. Genuinely caring about, and valuing teams, are the marks of a truly great modern leader............and will produce discretionary effort being given by those being led.

PETS AT HOME – A COLLABORATIVE LEADERSHIP STYLE

Speaking with Pets at Home, who have achieved strong placings in Britain's Great Places to Work survey, in the Sunday Times.........they articulated a collaborative leadership style. This could almost be interpreted as friendship rather than just an employer/employee relationship. The leadership style in Pets is spoken about in terms of being engaging and very much focussed on knowledge and detail...................but they are also honest in 'saying it like it is'.

Pets are very team based and collaborative, with successes and failures being owned by the team. The culture is non-political, and tends to reject individuals coming in with any 'political agenda'.

This collaborative culture and leadership style, has not only resulted in Best places to Work accolades, but also great commercial performance. Not bad for a private equity backed business!

INSTITUTE FOR EMPLOYMENT STUDIES
RESEARCH - INDICATES THAT STYLE MATTERS

I have been Chairman of the Board of IES for a number of years, and have total respect for the quality of their research into matters of employment. I wouldn't have devoted my time to Chairing the Board of IES if I didn't rate their research work.

IES research has indicated that leaders who are able to encourage their people..............are always clear about goals & expectations........and talk about how the individuals who work for them fit into the bigger picture of the overall goals of the organisation.

IES also found that great leaders were consistently good at the 'difficult stuff'. They were able to tackle poor performance quickly and effectively. They broke bad news well, and with integrity. The people who worked for these sort of leaders really appreciated their openness and honesty.

The IES research of great leaders consistently revealed, regardless of industry sector, nature of the work, seniority of the leader............that the following leadership behaviours are paramount:-

- Leaders who communicate well & make clear what is expected (no surprise there)
- Leaders who listen (no surprise there either), value and involve their teams in decisions
- Leaders who are supportive, and back up the team

- Leaders who show empathy and seek to understand
- Leaders who demonstrate and communicate a clear strategic vision
- Leaders who show an active interest in others (in other words – are able to treat people how they want to be treated)

These behaviours and characteristics are the polar opposite of some of the self-centred, egotistical leaders we have all worked with, or come across in working life.

Choosing an appropriate style of leadership for the organisation, which is fit for the modern world of today really matters. It matters particularly in terms of building a high performance culture.

ALDI – A CASE STUDY FOR CHOOSING A PARTICULAR LEADERSHIP STYLE

I was thinking about providing evidence for you, to show that choosing a different style of leadership results in change to business performance. I was chatting to my eldest son about this very topic. There are many potential exemplar organisations who have achieved high performance, but some might argue that their success was due more to other factors than just the chosen style of leadership. My son suggested the perfect example would be that of Aldi.

The rise of the discount food retailers in the U.K. food retail market has been widely documented. Many have charted the success of Aldi and Lidl against the big supermarkets, particularly during the major recession at the beginning of the 21st century. However, much less is known about the origins of Aldi.............and the fact that it is a perfect illustration of how much culture and the style of leadership trumps strategy.

There are now in existence globally, two Aldi businesses...........Aldi Nord (North) and Aldi Sud (South). Both carry exactly the same name, but the range and quality of products............and the shopping experience have diverged over time.

The history is that there were two founding Albrecht brothers – Theo (who died in 2010 aged 88) and Karl (who died in 2013 aged 94). They fell out with each other many years ago, over whether to sell cigarettes in their chain of stores. The consequence of this rift between the Albrecht brothers, was a decision to split the business geographically 50/50 between the two of them.

The geographical split between Aldi Nord (based in Essen in Germany) ran through Mulheim an der Ruhr, and Aldi Sud took the territory in south Germany below the line running through Mulheim an der Ruhr.

The Aldi story reveals that Theo was very traditional, with fairly entrenched thinking. He was somewhat reluctant to spend money as an individual, and consequently slow to innovate and learn. His style of leadership defined his part of the business. Aldi Nord stores feel small and claustrophobic.........somewhat disorganised, and lacking the ability to change and modernise.

The Albrecht brother Karl, who ran the Aldi Sud stores, was open to new ideas...........and became an innovator and change leader. His style built a far better culture in those southern stores, with a more modern and forward thinking management style. The two divided chains didn't compete in the same geography, but the commercial performance at Aldi Sud completely 'wiped the floor' with Aldi Nord over time. Aldi Sud has been consistently quicker to innovate and move with the times over the years. This was largely down to the fact that Karl was always more open minded as a leader than his brother Theo. They created two very different cultures in the same retail business, because of their chosen leadership styles.

In 2013, Aldi Sud grew by 7.8%, whilst Aldi Nord grew by a mere 2.9%. Aldi Sud has continued to expand to Switzerland and the U.S. Indeed, it is Aldi Sud which has stores very successfully established in the U.K.

With the founding fathers gone from the two businesses, many retail pundits are predicting an Aldi Sud takeover of Aldi Nord at some point. Surely, this is a classic case study proving that differences in chosen leadership style...........in exactly the same business ....lead to totally different commercial performance. Clearly culture does trump strategy.

TAKING A FRESH APPROACH TO YOUR LEADERSHIP STYLE IS BECOMING EVER MORE IMPORTANT

As I sit writing this book, an email has dropped into my inbox from the Chartered Institute of People &

Development.........which concerns the demands made by Generation Y individuals upon the leaders. The article talks about the fact that many of today's younger employees are highly educated professionals who want more of a 'business mentor' type of leader than has traditionally been the case. They are also choosing to work for businesses with a better culture.....it certainly features large in their employer selection criteria. Generation Y want to be able to enjoy their work. Workers are coming into organisations, who will not tolerate their working environment just for the sake of a pay packet. Culture and style of leadership is a real future differentiator.

The old style of 'carrot and stick' leadership has no attraction to Generation Y at all. They regard 'command and control' type leaders as old fashioned and divisive........with the vestiges of ineffective management tools (Annual Appraisals and other strict rules/ processes)......all of which come from an ever more obsolete management manual.

The CIPD article argues that the leader of today needs to recognise that people are more productive when they work in an atmosphere without fear, or even the promise of incentivised reward. Great leaders, in the modern era, are those able to nurture a style which creates strong internal culture and a collaborative environment. Such leaders make work enjoyable, because they understand that when people look forward to coming to work ....they are more loyal; committed; happy and energised. With this kind of leadership, people can grow in stature; relationships are encouraged to deepen;

productivity soars and people find new meaning and significance in their roles.

I couldn't put that better myself. I agree with every sentiment of the CIPD article. Except to say that I don't think this approach should be exclusive just to Generation Y. My own view is that all employees in the 21st century appreciate, and respond to this chosen style of leadership.

GURU & THINKER DAN PINK DOESN'T BELIEVE 'COMMAND & CONTROL' STYLE WORKS ANY LONGER EITHER

Management guru Dan Pink has attained a degree of notoriety in recent years. Dan's view is that 'command & control' management was first invented in the 1850s, in order to gain compliance in a 19th century industrial-ising world. It was good for then, and worked tolerably well in the 20th century. However, his view is that thinking is out of date for the 21st century.

Organisations are still using the old philosophy of "if-then" reward. "If you do this, then you get that". The trouble is, that kind of framework leads to a narrow focus, and stifles creativity & vision. Kodak was a case in point..............it met all its targets .... and made a brilliant job of being in the wrong busi-ness........making film for cameras, when the world was busy going digital. Dell hit all its numbers, but custom-ers were moving from P.C.s to tablet computers.

Doing things because we have always done them is a dangerous orthodoxy, and I agree with Dan Pink on this, that real creativity and flair originates from a much more modern and enabling style of leadership.

We live in a fast moving data rich, technology enabled world. Organisations today need to think about adopting a forward thinking and modern style of leadership ....which fits with the world in which we now operate.

"BUT WE HAVE A PRETTY GOOD STYLE OF LEADERSHIP IN OUR BUSINESS – DON'T WE?"

As a part of my work, I have the privilege of working with many leaders, in a variety of sectors, in organisations of all shapes and sizes. I regularly ask leaders to rate the style of leadership in their business. They generally tend to mark it above average. After all, such a question is partly asking how good they are themselves! Leaders rarely tell you that they're not good at leading others. I tend to equate it with admitting you're a bad driver........it's just not done very often.

Sadly, the survey statistics that regularly pass my desk, tell a completely different story. I've already quoted some disturbing statistics in the early part of this chapter..............and here are a few more.

47% of employees, in a recent survey thought they were being actively threatened by their manager. That's nearly half of all employees being bullied. The results were worse for the Civil Service; for scientists and also for doctors.

In a different survey, only 2% responded that they had high trust in their boss, with a third not trusting senior leadership generally. These are frightening statistics if they are representative of organisations generally. Also, they are an illustration which confirms that 'command & control' styles of leadership........based upon power, control, ego and profit are alive and well in the 21st century. I believe that such styles will cause businesses to seriously underperform their potential.

Yet another survey in 2015, showed 50% of people leave their job because of a bad boss, whilst only 45% thought their boss was good at growing the business. 40% thought line managers were ineffective, and in this same survey 37% felt they were being bullied.

I don't think I really need to go on quoting survey results for you. The pattern is clear. Leaders think they are generally ok. The workforce clearly says this is a bad case of 'the emperor's new clothes'. The leaders think they are clothed, the workers know and can see they are naked!!

AO.COM REPRESENTS A 'REFRESHINGLY MODERN' LEADERSHIP STYLE

I've already written about how much I admire what John Roberts has done through his leadership style at AO.com. His approach to leadership is refreshingly simple. He told me that there are very few rules in the business. John himself talks about principles, not pre-scriptions. One really great maxim which he uses with his people is "would your mum be proud of how you behaved? If the answer is yes, then do it. If the answer is no, then don't do it."

I love the simplicity of that maxim. Moreover, I can't see AO.com becoming a Kodak or a Dell. They are very much 'fleet of foot', and in tune with the modern leadership vibe of today. The concept of an appropriate leadership style isn't complex, but as a leader......you do have to be seen to walk your talk.

THE FOLLOWERS ARE WATCHING THE LEADERS – AND THEY DEMAND AUTHENTICITY

When Goffee and Jones (of London Business School) talked about followership in their book "Why should anyone be led you?" they recognised that followers want authentic leaders.

Followers can spot whether you are authentic or not pretty easily. If you don't keep your word; if you fail to do what you say you will do.......it's a deal breaker for followers. You are readily seen to not walk your talk. A bad failure, in the eyes of many followers, is to let people down when they need help. Worse still, followers are totally switched off if the leader takes credit for their work. Probably the ultimate leadership sin is to blame the team, and fail to provide 'air cover' for subordinates when pressure comes on. People will not forget that you let them down as a leader.

Followers want leaders who are calm in crisis; consistent in actions; who are trustworthy in keeping confidences and never seek to hand out blame. If we examine ourselves critically and honestly...............we may fall short of this 'gold standard' of follower expectations. I'm sure many of us have committed some leadership 'no-no's' at some time in our careers.

Never, by the way, be tempted to think that no one will notice when you slip from the required standard. As a leader, your behaviour and your words are constantly being monitored at all times. It's like being a famous celebrity watched by the paparazzi and the media. You as a leader are under the employee microscope at all times. Followers watch leaders.......it's an inescapable fact. They desperately want the 'best' version of who you can be.

Here is a cautionary story about being watched by employees. It's a U.S. example – so all U.K. leaders can relax – it's not about you (or could it be?) A newly appointed CEO walked around her offices in New York, meeting the senior team, and was given a guided tour of the building. As she walked around, she passed numerous of her employees and their workstations. She acknowledged no one; there was no eye contact; no nod of the head; no "how are you?" given to anyone...............other than the seniors to whom she was introduced.

Maybe this was a very daunting and nervous first day for the new CEO. Maybe she was by nature quite intro-verted? Maybe her office tour guide didn't know a lot of the names of some of the junior people either. None of these can be used as excuses. The point for leadership.............is that this first day walk around was a 'golden opportunity' missed. This particular business had recently made a number of redundancies, and there was a lot of uncertainty about the future. The CEO needed to take every possible opportunity to get the remaining people back on board – following her as the new leader of the business.

In not engaging with the ordinary people in her new place of work, the newly appointed CEO said so much about herself to the followers..............all without even speaking a word.

Remember, you as a leader, always live in an organisational 'goldfish bowl'. Followers are looking at you always, all the time. They miss nothing.

Leaders today need a 'new generation' approach to their leadership. If you are a leader......you need to be self-aware......in order to understand your effect upon others. Leaders need to be really careful not to switch off the potential discretionary effort of followers, by thoughtless behaviour. To be great, leaders need to be mindful of being watched. Key objectives in an organisation cannot be achieved without taking the tribe of followers with you.......and the best leaders know that well.

You could say that the essence of leadership revolves around those being led – and great leaders set the tone to build a healthy culture in which those being led can thrive. It's never just about what the leader achieves, but always more about what the followers achieve together. Great leadership is about connecting people

............not as in the New York CEO example. The great leader needs authenticity to connect the followers to the purpose of the organisation (and this needs to be more than just about making money). People working in organisations are keen to be a part of something worthwhile..............which is bigger than them-selves.....and is something of which they can be proud. The leader's job is to inspire a vision of shared mutual interest. When this happens, followers tend to give of their discretionary effort......they want to go the extra mile. This is the zone of the high performance culture...........and modern engaging leadership is critical to establishing and maintaining that environment.

WHAT THEN IS THE 'ESSENCE' OF A MODERN STYLE OF LEADERSHIP?

Most CEO groups I speak to will cite Winston Churchill as a figure from history whom they admire as a leader. Winston Churchill famously said; "the price of leader-ship is to stay positive, whether you feel like it or not". For Winston Churchill, a man with a tendency to depression (the 'black dog' as he called it), there was a clear personal cost to always appearing positive. For a Prime Minister leading a coalition Government during World War 2, when every battle was being lost, and almost everyone in the country thought Britain should sue for peace...........it was an incredible personal triumph to remain positive and urge the nation through the war effort. He was a truly remarkable leader, despite his many personal flaws.

My experience tells me that there is something very per-sonal that we put into leadership. As a leader, you must take what you have learned about the dos and don'ts of leadership, and set the tone for your organisation.

GERARD VAN GRINSVEN – AN INSPIRATIONAL AND CONNECTED LEADER

One of the CEOs I have had the pleasure to meet is Gerard van Grinsven. Gerard was a Ritz Carlton Hotel executive for a number of years, and he told me how that business became somewhat arrogant and detached from the customer. Executives were dressing in very fancy suits, and driving 'flash' cars, but customers were saying they were too stiff and not very family friendly. Ritz Carlton went through a period of re-listening to customers..........and consequent to that listening, began to regain market share once again.

At this time, Gerard recalls that he was the manager of the Ritz Carlton Oriental in Bangkok. It was a 5 star deluxe hotel, and by getting close to the customer, was voted 'Best hotel in the world' during the time he managed there.

Gerard recalls that he subsequently became CEO & President of the brand new $400m hospital in Detroit – the Henry Ford West Bloomfield Hospital. He took his lessons in leadership from the hospitality industry into his new CEO role, and tells how he was determined to put his own stamp on the hospital. He took an enlightened and very modern approach to both customer and employee relationships.

In setting up the new hospital, and in the operations going forward, Gerard chose to call new employees at

home, (on the day before they were due to start)............
to personally welcome them to the organisation. On
commencement day, he was there with his COO and
CFO to welcome new hires. This is extraordinary
.............and it sets the tone. Leaders always set the
tone. (Remember the CEO in New York who set the
tone badly). That is what great leadership is all
about................setting a tone you can be proud of,
and to which your people will respond positively.

Gerard's challenge to himself and his fellow leaders,
was to take an interest in his people.......not to be 'too
busy' to pay attention to their needs.

His learning from his days at Ritz Carlton, was to not
be absorbed by fancy titles, flash cars and well cut suits.
Gerard openly acknowledges that success is all about
culture. If the culture isn't right, you can demand what
you like..........but it won't happen. As CEO, Gerard
drives the culture of his hospital........he personally
ensures people are treated with dignity, because he
recognises they will then give their discretionary effort
to treat patients well.....and make the hospital
successful.

Interestingly, Gerard told me about how he also spent
time in the homes of potential customers in the commu-
nities of Detroit. He talked with families, ate with them,
and learned about their lives. He found out their opinions about what attracted them to use a particular hospital (remember in the U.S. you choose because you are
paying fees). He found out how important great food
was to the potential customers, and on the back of his

extensive customer conversations, he established the first ever culinary institute for healthcare in the U.S.

As a consequence of getting close to customers, Gerard provided a quality restaurant, and people in the community came to eat at the hospital restaurant. It has become a huge commercial driver of hospital revenues, and the hospital now even hosts wedding events............ it is that good! Gerard realised, by talking with people, that customers wanted more than just surgical excellence.....they wanted a total healing experience.......a major part of which was the food eaten during a hospital stay. Gerard realised this wasn't about clinicians taking the lead, but it was about personality and human relationships................in other words..........the culture of the place.

Gerard refused to hire 34 physicians, because (despite their eminent skills in medicine and impeccable qualifications) they didn't have the talent for creating great human relationships. Gerard wanted to hire great physicians who could actually relate to patients.

The leadership style is set by the leader. You put your own stamp on the business you are leading, by the personal style you inject. Gerard van Grinsven is a CEO who has taken his learning from his time at Ritz Carlton, and has taken his hospital in Detroit to No1 ranking in the U.S. Gallup survey for engagement. As a consequence of that leadership in establishing a healthy culture, his profitability and cash flow are excellent. His view is the same as mine........'culture trumps strategy'.......every time.

WHAT CHARACTERISTICS OF THE LEADER MAKE THE DIFFERENCE IN ESTABLISHING A HIGH PERFORMANCE CULTURE?

IES research in 2009 heard some very interesting commentary from people being led, about what they felt were great personal characteristics from their 'best bosses'.

"Listens to me, values me, involves me, and respects us."

"Is enthusiastic and inspiring."

"Is approachable."

"Is supportive and encouraging."

"Is open and honest."

"Takes a genuine interest in my development."

"Has strategic vision."

"Helps me achieve a good work/life balance."

"Is knowledgeable."

The 'follower' comments from that piece of IES research set a particular tone. It is strikingly similar to what Gerard van Grinsven was describing in the Detroit hospital story. Conversely, these statements are something the New York CEO failed to realise.

In many senses, far too much has been written about leadership in books over the years. Nevertheless, I would like to attempt to distil for you as the reader, a few thoughts about what really works in leadership style. I see some traits working time and time again, regardless of the personality of the individual manager. I don't want to give you a model, because circumstances alter cases. Some businesses require turnaround; others have a dubious leadership legacy which needs change ....others may be totally greenfield start ups like the Detroit hospital example. Some CEOs are introverts, whilst others are extroverts. Some CEOs are from a financial background, others come from marketing or commercial.

SO WHAT REALLY MATTERS IN GREAT LEADERSHIP?

Whatever the context of the enterprise, and whoever you are as an individual leader & personality, I believe there are a few really important actions in establishing your style of leadership.............so here is my list of 7 things:-

  i. Direction/Purpose/Vision/Inspiration
      A great leader takes you to a place you wouldn't have gone on your own. This is part of that inspirational quality to cause you to believe what you at first thought wasn't possible. It always involves communicating a purpose which means more to followers than just making money alone.
  ii. Risk Taking
      True leaders are prepared to take calculated risks to achieve real gains. There is convincing evidence in a survey of 19,000 employees (by the Corporate

Leadership Council), that a risk taking culture is the top factor in energising and motivating employees. We like to be in an organisation where the leaders are trying new things and going to places that 'no one has gone before' to quote the Star Trek phrase! There are plenty of examples where businesses were not taking risks.......... Kodak has already been mentioned....but I could include Woolworths; Nokia; Kwik Save; HMV; British Leyland; Little Chef; City Link; Austin Reed and many others.

Great leaders take real risks and are prepared to be unpopular in doing so. They ignore the status quo, and thereby set an inspiring vision. They see real opportunity when others are uncertain. Risk is a key enabler of success.

iii. Accountability

Leaders are specific with expectations and hold people accountable. This involves doing what is right, rather than taking the popularity route. Wanting to be liked can be a real barrier to authentic leadership. A great leader never runs from confrontation...........and always pursues doing the right thing.

iv. Being human – showing your weaknesses

A great leader will always talk about their weaknesses before anyone else does. True leaders show emotions. It's actually ok to be frustrated; to celebrate and recognise effort above the norm. Great bosses use their humanity to inspire others. Above all.....be your real self........or you can never be authentic, and will be seen as a phoney.

v. Giving 'air cover' to followers
Leadership, at its best, is about protecting those who work for you. Giving 'air cover' to subordinates......allowing them the space to perform ....giving them the credit for the wins, and being prepared to take the blame on their behalf for anything that goes wrong. I always found in my corporate career that was massively appreciated by those who worked for me. Bad leaders always blame others.

vi. 'Killing off' the status thing
True leaders do not behave in an entitled way. They are never too far above themselves to roll up their sleeves, get 'down and dirty' and do real work. They regularly go 'back to the floor' so that they can understand the basics, and learn what works and what doesn't work. Great leaders don't use position power to get things done. They lead by showing followers their contribution and style..........and people then want to be led by them. People need to feel that 'we are all in this together'.

vii. Thanking people – recognition matters
All great leaders say thank you well. (I will be covering this as a separate chapter later) they look for situations to catch people doing things right and recognise them. Saying thank you appropriately is so basic, yet so powerful. Recognition, done well, produces higher performance in everyone, and inspires them to give discretionary effort.

So......................may I ask the question.........."
what does it feel like to be led by you?" If you gave

yourself a score out of 10.............where 10 is the gold standard for world class leadership in those 7 character-istics..............how do you think you would fare? Why not try asking some of your most respected employees to rate your leadership against those head-ings. Make it anonymous and ask a representative sample. Are you brave enough to ask? Would you be pleasantly surprised, or a little deflated?

SUMMARY POINTS:

- Leadership style matters
- The Aldi case study shows 2 halves of the same business were separated by style – and performance followed culture
- In the modern world – command & control doesn't work well
- Followers demand an authentic modern and engaging style
- You are probably not as good a leader as you think!

YOUR ACTION – TEST YOUR LEADERSHIP CAPABILITY:

Here are 7 questions to ask your selected sample of employees by anonymous pulse survey:-

1. Have I provided an inspiring vision for where we are heading. Are you excited by the challenge?
2. Are we taking risks under my leadership which will transform our future performance capability?
3. Do I do what is right and hold everyone to account? Do I take the tough calls when required?
4. Do I show humility, reveal my weaknesses........... in short....is my leadership the real authentic me?
5. Do I protect the team, give you credit for your work.......and take the hit if blame is handed to us?
6. Do I roll up my sleeves and work with you, and lead less because of my position, and more because you respect me.
7. Do I regularly thank people for a job well done?

Take the test................leadership matters!!!

Be the brave leader who asks for feedback. Leadership style matters...........it sets the tone..............it establishes the culture

Chapter 10

Managing People's Performance

DEALING WITH UNDERPERFORMANCE AND PUSHING YOUR TALENT

"Our culture is friendly and intense, but if push comes to shove, we'll settle for intense." Jeff Bezos CEO Amazon

"Performance more often comes down to cultural challenge, rather than simply a technical one." Lara Hogan, Etsy

"It is no use saying that we are doing our best. You have to succeed at doing what is necessary." Winston Churchill

"If you are building a culture where honest expectations are communicated & peer accountability is the norm, then the group will address poor performance and attitudes." Henry Cloud

"Executives owe it to the organisation and to their fellow workers, not to tolerate nonperforming individuals in important jobs." Peter Drucker

WHY IS MANAGING THE PERFORMANCE OF PEOPLE SO IMPORTANT?

Managing the performance of people is the 'Achilles heel' of many CEOs that I meet. They tell me that they are working hard on communication and recognition; they are thinking about leadership style..............but they freely admit they find dealing with underperformance problems difficult.

Sometimes, this reluctance to deal with underperformance is because we have worked with people for a long time. We know them well..........sometimes we know their family well, and tackling their shortcomings can be both difficult and embarrassing.

More importantly, many executives tell me they just dislike facing into a conflict situation. Sometimes this is the fear of causing potential costly litigation (by getting the process wrong), but really it is more often the conflict avoidance itself. U.K. executives are about as far removed from the Alan Sugar 'Apprentice' programme stereotype ("You're fired"), as it is possible to be.

NOT FACING INTO ISSUES OF UNDERPERFORMANCE HAS A HUGE NEGATIVE EFFECT ON OVERALL WORKFORCE MORALE

We should all be aware that underperforming or difficult people will become more of a morale problem with the passage of time. The issue becomes embedded, and more immovable in the organisation..........and the effect upon other co-workers is to diminish their performance..........in a sometimes dramatic and certainly corrosive way. No performance management problem, if unresolved, is an island.

The problem people who we don't deal with effectively and quickly, will downgrade the morale and performance of everyone who has visibility of the situation. People begin to 'mutter' behind the scenes about "why should I care, when X is not being dealt with?" If the problem person is a senior or Board figure, then not only may they be affecting performance negatively, they may also be causing labour turnover of some of your best people. People leave bad leaders, rather than companies.

THE BEST LEADERS ARE ABLE TO USE 'TOUGH LOVE'

If people, despite our best efforts to help them make the grade.......do not get there...........then it becomes time for them to move on elsewhere. The best leaders do this.....recognise this as a skill which can be acquired, and also something that can be done well. Showing 'tough love' and helping people to move on with their self-respect intact............can ultimately lead to that problem person being much happier elsewhere, doing something more suited to their skills or personality. The leader taking the action should set out into the process with the objective of having a relationship with the problem individual after removing them from their role. Done well, this is entirely possible.

TAKING EFFECTIVE ACTION ON UNDERPERFORMANCE LIFTS MORALE

Never lose sight of the fact that tackling one of those 'immovable' problems...........people who have been around for years but are a performance or behavioural issue............will have a dramatic effect on the morale and performance of everyone who has visibility of the issue. The organisation will almost feel as if it has breathed a sigh of relief that someone has had the temerity to tackle the issue. Employees always admire the leader who is an effective performance management exponent. It is a fairly rare and much appreciated skill.

JAMES TIMPSON – A ROLE MODEL FOR PROACTIVE PERFORMANCE MANAGEMENT

I have already cited the Timpson business as an employer I much admire for their culture, and they are also good at performance management. James Timpson, the CEO, says they are ruthless at removing people who don't fit the culture, because he believes it's only fair to other colleagues who do fit.

James talked about a period in the Timpson head office, where they removed quite a few people who just didn't 'get' the culture. He speaks about a 10 year journey to face into issues around managing performance, and grow a high performance culture. The Timpson business today has a weekly notification of any 'colleagues of concern', and believes in moving quickly regarding the issue of underperforming people. I think this has to be one of the requirements of a high performance culture. Your people need to know that there is real accountability for everyone.

As Winston Churchill so succinctly put it; "it's no use saying you're doing your best. You have to succeed at doing what is necessary."

JOHN ROBERTS AT AO.COM – PERFORMANCE MANAGEMENT ALIGNED WITH THE CUSTOMER

John Roberts, as CEO of AO.com is just as vociferous as James Timpson on the topic of managing people's performance. He told me that if you are rude to any one of his customers, you will automatically be fired. There are no exceptions. John says the culture is kind and caring, but will not tolerate any form of bad customer treatment.

John Roberts has built a culture where he does lots of great things for his people.............and the list of those things is long........but at the same time he doesn't suffer fools gladly. He is extremely tough on the delivery driver/customer interface. He knows that is a key 'touch point' for impressing customers, and getting word of mouth for onward customer recommendation. Every quarter, the business reviews driver performance, and removes the bottom 5%. As CEO, he writes to every customer who makes a complaint personally. If a driver is mentioned in a customer complaint, they get a yellow card, and that is part of the criteria for assessing the bottom 5% who will leave. Writing customer letters personally keeps John in touch with the day to day performance management of the business................ which he regards as vital.

SO – WHAT IS EFFECTIVE MANAGEMENT OF THE PERFORMANCE OF YOUR PEOPLE?

Really effective performance management means that your people know exactly what they should be doing (and how their bit of the action fits within the overarching business objectives); knowing what they're good at; knowing how and where they need to focus; where they might need to get better (including how they might achieve that) and what support they have to do all that.

The management of performance, in a high performance culture, is a collaborative employer and employee discussion of both past and current performance, and sharing expectations for the immediate future. This kind of dialogue should be regular, and it should be very much 'business as usual'.

What effective performance management is not ....is a diplomatic euphemism for putting people into a disciplinary 'slippery slope' process................ nor is it merely some ritualistic annual form filling appraisal process.

Really good management of the performance of your people should be an intrinsic part of your culture for everyone. Great leaders know this is a key tool in their armoury to achieving the organisation's aims, goals and objectives. Poor leaders see this as a process............an 'add on' imposed by the business which wastes their time for real work. They will be far less effective in striving for a high performance culture...........because they are not utilising what is available to them.

THERE IS A MAJOR SEISMIC SHIFT TAKING PLACE IN THE MANAGEMENT OF PEOPLE'S PERFORMANCE

Huge numbers of businesses are currently examining, and potentially thinking of changing their formal performance management processes. Over 65% of U.K. firms are looking to change the way they conduct the management of people's performance.

Thinking globally, Microsoft and Google have both abandoned the dreaded 'Annual Appraisal', replacing it with much more frequent informal reviews.

In all my business experience, I have yet to meet either a leader or an employee who enjoys, or finds amazing value in Annual Appraisal processes. People criticise the documentation. People also criticise the principle of Annual Appraisal itself. Everyone openly acknowledges that trying to assess performance once per year is extraordinarily difficult, and ultimately of little merit. At its worst, it can be hugely counterproductive.

Inefficient processes (of which the Annual Appraisal is but one) contribute to dwindling productivity levels around the world. Over 25% of people report in surveys that confusion at work (through unclear goals & expectations) repeatedly contribute to them wasting time and missing targets.

The more enlightened CEOs are amongst those who want to invest time and technology in becoming more productive. As you read this book, I wonder if you are one of those enlightened leaders who wants to change the process for the better?

Despite the fact that almost every leader would agree that performance reviews are often defective, abolition is not the answer.

A piece of research of 9,000 leaders & employees, across 18 countries, by technology firm CEB, found that most respondents thought that a complete overhaul of backward looking, inconsistent and over-complex performance review processes was required. However, that same piece of research revealed that those organisations who had dropped formal review processes altogether...........had subsequently experienced a significant drop in productivity! So the answer in not to abandon every form of review of performance.

The CEB survey found performance dropped by an average of 10% without reviews of any kind. Moreover, the effect on high performers was even more negative ....28% of them felt undervalued..............so the people who most want to be appraised in some way are your top performers (they obviously view appraisal as part of their recognition that someone is noticing them). Having no evaluation at all also showed up in the survey as a driver of labour turnover, due to the fact there was no relationship between pay rises and performance.

So the answer to unpopular appraisal processes is not to replace them with a vacuum. I believe the answer is really simple.

REGULAR INFORMAL REVIEWS ARE THE EASY ANSWER TO GREAT PERFORMANCE MANAGEMENT

The executives running the likes of Microsoft and Google are not stupid. They have indeed abandoned the Annual Appraisal as a useless piece of management bureaucracy. But they obviously need to be fast moving and highly productive businesses. They have moved their reviews to regular informal one to one feedback sessions.

Research by Right Management U.K. recommends exactly the same practice. Moving from annual review, to monthly catch ups, where clear goals can be agreed with line managers, can help employees feel more engaged, productive and happier. Views on the performance of the individuals are current and therefore relevant, and objectives can be amended in tune with the dynamic changes in the business. If you have 12 informal reviews, as a part of your normal one to one meetings with your line manager, it is bound to be less of a big deal...............and therefore less negative and conflicted. The individual will not feel pressed into an unreal 'defend or die' annual meeting.

WHITBREAD GROUP GO BI-MONTHLY WITH THEIR REVIEWS

Whitbread have moved from the old style Annual Appraisals, and now review the performance of their people every 2 months.

This has been successful in weeding out and removing underperformers..........and showing an overall improvement in both morale and productivity. Regular reviews really do work. Once a year is far too long to expect any positive impact upon productivity.............. it is largely irrelevant to current performance, and a ritual with little validity.

NETFLIX HAS CONSIGNED ANNUAL APPRAISAL TO THE 'LANDFILL' OF BUREAUCRACY

Netflix believes Annual Appraisals to be a waste of time, and much prefers its approach of getting managers and employees to engage in conversations about performance as an organic part of their day to day work.

Their approach is to hire people who will be self-starters (hire for attitude); to free them from the bureaucracy of form filling.......and to require outperformance from everyone. They are open in stating that average performance will merit a severance package. Poor performers get no credit for their hard work.......it is results which count in the Netflix culture. B level performance, no matter how great the effort, is shown the door.

At Netflix, there are regular informal conversations between the individual and the leader, and once per year personal development plans are drawn up. Appraisal (certainly the Annual Form filling) has disappeared.

The Netflix model may be too big a leap for your organisation, but all the evidence points to the fact that regular reviews are the key to fluidity; relevance and increased morale/productivity. Why wouldn't you want to try something which involves less effort, and increases the productivity and morale of your people? At the same time, you would be removing a management ritual (Annual Appraisal) which manager and employee alike all loathe.

IS IT TIME TO GIVE UP ANNUAL PERFORMANCE APPRAISALS COMPLETELY?

A U.S. poll of 3,000 people showed that 98% felt annual performance reviews were unnecessary, but only 6% of U.S. firms had dropped them at that stage.

The U.K. picture is a similar one. CIPD research in 2009 showed 80% of firms carrying out an annual appraisal process. Yet the IES report of 2011 found annual appraisal is viewed as an administrative process.

It seems that almost all the commentators I have read agree that a once per year meeting on this important topic is not enough. Performance management should be a summary of regular day to day conversations. The best people you employ want regular feedback to drive their performance further...........but so does everyone else you employ.

The organisations with more informal cultures, seem to be more adept at regular one to one conversations dealing with performance. This can only be a good thing, and leads to healthy dialogue.

Many executives are actually thinking about changing their clunky annual appraisal systems. However, lack of actual action means that annual appraisal is far from dead yet!

A study by E.Reward in 2011 found that although 74% of organisations had made changes to their appraisal processes over the previous 3 years, the majority of respondents remained dissatisfied, and further changes were planned.

Too many managers still think of appraisal as a painful, lengthy once per year process..........one which they could well do without. The key is to change to a culture of regular effective one to one conversations about performance, and to keep objectives moveable as the business changes.

CAN PERFORMANCE MANAGEMENT WORK IN DIFFICLUT ENVIRONMENTS? AN NHS CASE STUDY

I rarely use the NHS as an exemplar of organisational excellence, but Michael West of Aston University found that there was a strong correlation between high quality performance management, and healthcare outcomes in 52 hospitals, (especially in respect of patient mortality). You cannot have more serious stakes in performance than the life or death of patients.

It is always more important to focus on the quality of conversations in the workplace, and for line managers to have the necessary skill to carry out quality discussions with individuals. There should be much less focus therefore, on forms and form filling.

One could ask the question.......why performance management has such an image problem with leaders, and there is so much moaning about the inconvenience...........when it can be so influential..............and in this NHS example........a matter of the difference between life and death outcomes?

I believe it is time for leaders to 'step up to the plate' on the subject of effective management of people's performance.

IES RESEARCH IN 2012 IDENTIFIED 10 'TOP TIPS' FOR SUCCESSFUL PERFORMANCE MANAGEMENT

As a leader, you may be realising that you should do something about your own 'clunky' performance management capability.

But what should you be thinking of doing specifically? The IES (where I am Chairman – as I have previously mentioned) did some research work on this topic in 2012. They came up with 10 'top tips' for implementing effective performance management in your business. I include them for your consideration:-

i. <u>Position performance management in terms of managing performance all year round</u>
   - Regularity of review conversations is key
   - Set out priorities in one to ones
   - Give feedback on progress (good & bad) regularly
ii. <u>Prioritise motivating performance & development conversations for all employees</u>
   - Performance management is for everyone
   - It's not just for poor/top performers
   - Quality of one to one conversations is vital
iii. <u>Keep the system simple/stable</u>
   - Make it easy to do – how hard can it be?
   - Don't fiddle with it
   - Set objectives/give feedback/agree action

iv. <u>Technology can support but should not drive</u>
- Putting it online may help
- Power is still in the quality of the conversations
- Again the mantra must be – make it easy

v. <u>Objective setting is about business alignment</u>
- Work priorities change – discuss regularly
- Make sure people know what to do – latest
- Make sure priorities align to the big picture

vi. <u>Any link to pay needs to be simple & transparent</u>
- Again – keep it simple
- Summarise at regular reviews where/how individual performance is

vii. <u>Clarify & emphasise development actions</u>
- All employees (excellent/average/poor performers) should be having support conversations
- Development actions should be relevant to the individual and to the overall organisation

viii. <u>Support managers in dealing with persistent poor performers</u>
- Some employees 'play games' & do just enough to survive until the next conversation
- Managers need help to 'weed out' those playing the system

ix. <u>Clarify the rules of appraiser and appraise</u>
- Managers should conduct good one to one conversations
- Employees should come to the table well prepared

x. <u>Performance management training should be given</u>
- The best organisations train management in this key skill

PERFORMANCE MANAGEMENT OVER EMPHASISES POOR PERFORMERS – DON'T FORGET YOUR BEST TALENT

The emphasis in this Chapter on managing performance has tended to focus on the underperformers, and how to effectively manage them. This is natural, because of seeking solutions to the natural tendency for leaders to avoid conflict.

However, managing talent should be a real pleasure for all leaders, by comparison with managing conflict. I have had many conversations with leaders about whom they are 'bringing on' in the business. We must not forget that our regular performance management should play to the recognition and development of our top talent.

Leaders should organise to give early opportunities for rising stars, and support them to develop even further in their careers. I have already alluded to the fact that the one group of employees who are keen to be reviewed, is the top performing group of employees. They view performance appraisal as part of their own recognition, which confirms to them that the organisation is noticing their efforts.

A study by technology firm Ricoh found that 67% of employees in the 18-26 age bracket were working long hours, in order to try to impress their bosses. Presenteeism seems to be alive and well in the upcoming generation of technology workers, and gives some indication that business entrants are keen to do well and make career progress. We need to take care as leaders not to switch off their enthusiasm by poor and outdated performance management processes.

We owe it to our best talent, but also to all our employees, to have regular conversations with them................. which keeps their work dynamically aligned to the ever changing needs of the business. We also need to give them feedback to the perennial question in every employee's head........"How am I doing?"

I believe we also need to say "impress me by your outputs.......rather than by how long or hard you work."

SUMMARY POINTS:

- Are you leading your organisation to face into managing people's performance?
- Do you exercise 'tough love' where necessary?
- Do your people have regular reviews of objectives, which constantly adjust to align with the overall objectives and aims of the organisation?
- Do people know how they are doing on a regular basis?
- Will you review your performance appraisal system to make it simple; informal; frequent and relevant?
- Are you going to train leaders in the skill of having great performance conversations?

YOUR ACTIONS:

What action do you think is necessary on managing performance in your organisation?

Will you review your business against the IES 10 top tips?

CHAPTER 11

The Power Of Recognition
In Developing A Motivational Culture

SAYING A SINCERE 'THANK YOU' IS ALL IT TAKES

"Money motivates neither the best performers nor the best in people. Purpose does." @nilofer

"Dispirited, unmotivated, unappreciated workers cannot compete in a highly competitive world." Francis Hesselbein

"The simple act of paying positive attention to people has a great deal to do with productivity." Tom Peters

"It is crucial to recognise, reward and celebrate accomplishments." Rosabeth Kanter

"Find people who look for the best in others, lavish more praise than criticism, and love what they do." Richard Branson

"Celebrate what you want to see more of." Tom Peters

> "Research indicates workers have 3 prime needs; interesting work; recognition for doing a good job and being let in on things that are going on in the company." Zig Ziglar
>
> "Appreciate everything your people do for the business. Nothing else can quite substitute for a few well chosen, well timed, sincere words of praise. They're absolutely free, and worth a fortune." Sam Walton

WHY THE OBSESSION WITH MONEY?

We have obsessed about remuneration, almost to the exclusion of any other factors in seeking to recognise and reward individual performance in organisations.

Frederick Irving Herzberg wrote about the motivation of people as far back as the 1950s, so this subject is not exactly new. I remember learning as a very young manager, that Herzberg had said that money was a 'dis-satisfier', and that you would spend much of your time figuring out, in the realms of remuneration, how to be as fair as possible..........and how to reduce or mitigate potential negativity toward monetary reward. I wonder how many remuneration committees realise that this is their real role in life?

In 2015, the Co-Chief Executive of Deutche Bank, John Cryan said that bankers were paid too much for simply handling other people's money. He was even critical of his own level of remuneration! Pay does need to support a reasonable lifestyle according to skill and results achieved. There is also some face validity, in expecting that brain surgeons will be paid more than road sweepers.

However, research by Gallup and the psychologist Daniel Kahneman put that acceptable amount of remuneration at £50,000 per annum in 2015; finding that earnings over that amount derived no additional happiness. This piece of research also found that for people who earned more than this level who were in fact happier, did not agree that monetary reward was the reason for their positivity.

I regularly encounter CEOs and Directors in businesses, who tell me that really it's all about money. My firm belief is that Herzberg was right, it is definitely not all about money. How on earth does the voluntary sector work, if it is all about money?

The Institute of Leadership and Management (ILM), found that bonuses are not the top motivator for employees......in a 2013 study looking into what makes employees productive. Their findings suggested that £36.9billion spent per annum on performance bonuses in the U.K., had no impact on the motivation and commitment levels of the vast majority of recipients! The ILM survey highlighted how important it was that managers were good at ensuring how happy and motivated their people were. When asked what one thing would motivate them more/or get them to do more; 31% of employees said "more praise and a greater sense of being valued." That is a significant response...........and we should take notice!!

THE POWER OF RECOGNITION AS A MOTIVATOR

We do have a productivity problem as a nation. Statistics suggest our productivity is 20% below the average in the G7 nations, and yet employers constantly tell me they are striving for productivity.

All the research would suggest that the way to get better productivity is not exclusively about money. There is a wealth of evidence to suggest that employee engagement and a strong culture is a major lever in driving better performance. Research in 2015, conducted by Bill Alexander, CEO of Red Letter Days for business, suggested the importance of recognition for achievement in the workplace.

It seems common sense to me that employees need to feel appreciated. Being thanked for a job well done, by the boss whom you report to, has a massive effect upon your well-being, your self-respect and subsequently your motivation for future performance. The praise has to be real, authentic and sincere. It has to be based upon proper measures of success, and must have not a 'whiff' of favouritism. If it passes those tests, and you merely thank people, it will have a disproportionately positive impact.

How many major levers for motivation and productivity do you know that are totally free? I suspect your answer may be....."none." I believe that we downgrade recognising and appropriately thanking people in our own minds....simply because these things are free. How wrongheaded that is. It may be counter-intuitive to think that saying "thank you" is hugely valuable........that doesn't change the fact that research says it is true.

LEADERS NEED TO REALISE HOW
THE HUMAN BRAIN IS 'WIRED'

Matthew Lieberman's book 'Social – why our brains are wired to connect', delves into the belief of scientists studying the impact of positive feedback on people ....by scanning their brains as they read praise in letters about them from random people. The research clearly indicates that (whilst many firmly believe that money is the biggest motivator) recognition is much more powerful. In the research, people were very willing to trade (give up) cash payments in return for letters of praise!!

A further scientific study of the human brain, conducted in Japan during 2015 by Keise Izuma also suggested that people crave positive feedback. Even when participants in this study received fairly low-level positive feedback, there was activation in the reward areas of the brain.

Taking these scientific brain activity findings............. which were both based upon fairly trivial low level positive feedback, just imagine the power of applying this in the real world.........where the praise was for real work.....and made by a significant leader in your hierarchy. The power to move the mind and motivation of the individual is enormous.

WHY DO WE NOT NOTICE GOOD PERFORMANCE AND THEN RECOGNISE IT REGULARLY?

One phenomenon that fascinates me, is that we are almost hard-wired in leadership roles to focus on business problems, in very precise detail. You could, no doubt, articulate your biggest current business concern; when it began; who has been involved so far; and what you believe needs to happen next. I don't believe you would need to refer to any documentation to describe the problem......it would all be in your head......and in some detail.

Conversely, if I asked you to tell me what had gone particularly well in the business lately, then you would probably have something in mind, but it would be in far less detail than the big troubling problem. We are not in the habit of noticing the behaviour of others which deserves praise.................and we certainly don't have the command of the detail we use on problem situations. Things have gone well, so we don't need to focus. Consequently, we don't have the tools to give detailed relevant praise to those responsible for success.

Getting the detail of what is going well in the organisation.....taking note of it.......finding out exactly who is responsible (individual or team), and thanking them in public with their peers......will have extraordinarily powerful motivational results. Why not try this for yourself...........and do it with accuracy and authenticity. You may well be surprised at the power it produces.

WHICH COMPANIES ARE WORKING INNOVATIVELY WITH RECOGNITION TO MOTIVATE THEIR PEOPLE?

As I travel around the world of business and organisations, I constantly encounter stories of CEOs who are doing some excellent work around the recognition of their people. They are startling advocates for the positive effect upon the performance of their people..........
and resultant productivity.

TIMPSON'S ROLLS ROYCE AND THEIR HOLIDAY HOMES

I have already written about the culture James Timpson is building in a number of chapters of this book. James told me that he is personally committed to the power of recognition of outperformance of his people. He puts time and effort into this very important area.

He told me that Timpson have decided on a scheme for anyone nominated as 'employee of the month' (which obviously has criteria and judging of nominations) ....where the winner gets the use of the company Rolls Royce for a month. That sort of recognition is a real 'wow' for the proud recipient. Not surprisingly, this has been both a novel and powerful piece of recognition. This is not only a big deal in the workplace, but also in the community in which those employees live. Employees really want to win for a month, and when they do............the neighbours see their success visually. The Rolls Royce scheme is a powerful reminder of the kind of culture James is building at Timpson.

James took another recognition idea from a niche electronics retailer..... Richer Sounds......a tip passed on by Julian Richer. Timpson purchased some holiday homes for recognising various aspects of outperformance by employees. Again, the significance of free holiday accommodation, recognising a job really well done....is far more memorable and long lasting than simple monetary reward.

These 'set pieces' of recognition are powerful symbols .....totems if you like.....that the Timpson business appreciates what people do on the job.............and believes in saying a very public "thank you."

'FILLING UP YOUR BUCKET' – RECOGNITION AT GALLUP

Gallup, the polling organisation, firmly believes that negativity is a massive threat to company performance.

Gallup gives employees a bucket to sit on their desk/workstation, and people are encouraged to put handwritten notes (notice....not emails......email junkies please take note) praising people for performance/behaviour that is above and beyond, into other employee's buckets.

This is a very visible method of showing appreciation for a job well done. Gallup would also say that people who fill other people's buckets frequently, tend to get reciprocal thank you's back. Recognition behaviour leads to reciprocity at Gallup. That is a healthy positive for their culture.

THE POWER OF THE HANDWRITTEN NOTE - TO YOUR HOME AT PEPSICO

I know people personally, who have a handwritten note from their CEO which they have retained from 25 years ago............and it still has meaning for them. They tell me they will keep it always.

Indra Nooyi, the Chair/CEO of Pepsico, sent letters to the parents of her top teams. She realised how her own achievements had made her mother very proud, and wanted to 'tap into' a similar rich vein of family pride.

Indra continues to send handwritten notes (email junkies – please take note yet again.....email doesn't hack it in recognition) to the husbands and wives of her outstanding performers. Imagine the household conversations amongst Pepsico employees and their families. The effect on motivation, and the sense of pride when the letter comes to the home................saying how well you have done & what you have achieved. Indra believes this is hugely powerful, and she is right.

Is this 'too American' for your tastes? Why not try it before you dismiss the idea. I would respectfully suggest you might be very surprised by the effect.

'ACTION MAN SELFIES' AT KFC – NOW THAT'S REALLY OVER THE TOP!!

KFC achieved Top employer U.K. certification in 2013, and one element of that success they were particularly proud of, was allowing all their managers to choose their own personal recognition award to give to their people.

James Watts, Vice President of human resources (we will have to forgive him for having a poor job title), told People Management Magazine that his personal favourite recognition technique was an Action Man super hero figure – which he puts into a Usain Bolt 'victory pose' and takes a picture of the people who have done a fantastic job in living the culture...............they pose together with the figure for the picture (boss and employee)..............and Awards from James and other Directors are posted on KFCs internal social media site each week. Apparently, this has gone down a storm with KFC employees.

This may be a little too gimmicky for you, but the generation Y workforce at KFC love that kind of thing. I think the learning from this example is not to be too formal or 'stiff & starchy' about the principle of recognition. KFC are saying 'thank you' in a zany 'off the wall' kind of way...............and for them, it drives the right kind of behaviour and performance. This whole recognition idea has grown a life of its own at KFC, and many employees share it with friends and family via social media..............as a demonstration of their pride in their own performance achievements.

'CEO OWNERSHIP' OF THE RECOGNITION PRINCIPLE - AT COFFEE CHAIN - CAFFE NERO

Caffe Nero has seen a long period of double digit growth, with employee numbers growing by a factor of

9 times over the same period. They have concentrated heavily on engaging their employees from the top down.

Their belief is that the CEO should communicate the vision (communicate, communicate, communicate), whilst seeking feedback from their people (systematic listening). As people apply themselves to that vision from the CEO, the business thinks it is vital that they be recognised and acknowledged. Nero's CEO wants employees to feel special, because the business realises that at least 50% of their customers visit the coffee shops because of the attitude of the employees, as much as the coffee products themselves. Service is always part of any buying experience, and great service needs to be recognised to keep it vibrant and fresh.

WHY DOES RECOGNITION MATTER SO MUCH?

It is my observation, and the view expressed by so many case studies, that organisations with employees who display pride and enthusiasm, always outperform competitors who fail to nurture the enthusiasm of their people........by recognising outperformance.

Even the recent past Governor of the Bank of England, Mervyn King observed "motivation does not come from financial incentives alone.....the financial sector has done us a disservice in promoting the belief that massive financial compensation is necessary to motivate individuals." I believe that is a true statement. We have become misguided.......because recognition is relatively free, we discount it as having relatively little value. Nothing could be further from the truth in the real world.

Goffee & Jones, of the London Business School, expressed the view that "if companies organised more to draw on, and fuel the enthusiasms of people, and less to maximise efficiency, the problem of disengagement would be gone forever."

Leaders need to 'wake up and smell the coffee' on this fundamental principle......recognition is free, and yet has a massive effect on human well-being; self-respect and performance. How many big levers on human performance do you know that are low- to no cost......and yet hugely effective? Recognition matters.

Statistics from Globoforce, tell us that companies with effective recognition mechanisms have 31% lower voluntary turnover than those who do not. Also, 64% of employees from their data, say that they would move to an organisation that clearly recognises the contributions of employees. Recognition matters!

**CONCLUSIONS OF THE GALLUP ENGAGEMENT SURVEY FROM 10 MILLION RESPONDENTS..........
THAT'S A LOT OF DATA!!**

The Gallup organisation worldwide survey of 10 million employees led them to produce 12 key employee expectations........which boil down to how employees 'feel' at work. This is expressed in terms of relationships with colleagues and managers; whether they feel they are being listened to; and if they are encouraged & praised at work.

This study resulted in the now widely known and used Gallup 12. I wonder............how would your employees fare in answering these questions?

1. I know what is expected of me at work.
2. I have the materials & equipment I need to do my work right.
3. At work, I have opportunity to do what I do best every day.
4. In the last 7 days, I have received recognition or praise for good work.
5. My supervisor, or someone at work, seems to care about me as a person.
6. There is someone at work who encourages my development.
7. At work, my opinions seem to count.
8. The mission/purpose of my company makes me feel my job is important.
9. My associates or fellow employees are committed to doing quality work.
10. I have a best friend at work.
11. In the last 6 months, someone has talked to me about my progress.
12. This last year, I have had opportunities to learn & grow.

Question 4 of the Gallup 12 is quite challenging. It means that weekly, someone needs to recognise your contribution. That's quite a hurdle for many workplaces!

My belief is that we spend too little time as leaders recognising and thanking people for what they do. I've heard so many line managers utter that terrible phrase "well, they get paid to do their job, don't they?" What a Neanderthal belief that is. Even worse, we often believe a pay rise will fix many of the ills! How very wrong that belief is also.

Between 2000 and 2006, the average pay for Doctors doubled (yes doubled!), but statistics showed that they were no happier than before. The same could be said for many other professions, where pay levels are high, yet satisfaction and happiness levels are low. It seems counterintuitive...................yet statistical data seems to show that individuals are satisfied by sufficient pay to live on.....yet beyond that amount.........motivation comes from other factors. It's no real surprise to those who know Maslow's hierarchy of needs. We are 'self-actualised' by non-monetary factors.

Money does not buy happiness. Recognition is vitally important for the self-actualisation of individuals. It is high time that leaders changed their 'head furniture' in this vital area.............because of overwhelming evidence that recognition matters. Will you as the reader..........and leader of your organisation/team be willing to experiment in this area?

SUMMARY POINTS:

- Are you obsessed with outdated beliefs about money and motivation in the workplace?
- Do you realise the power of recognition to motivate your people?
- Do you now understand how the human brain is 'hard-wired' to require praise?
- Can you begin to track and recognise individual outperformance in the detailed way you track problems?
- Will you as the CEO 'own' the principle of recognition and role model doing it?

YOUR ACTIONS:

How would your employees fare in completing the Gallup 12..............and especially Question 4 about weekly recognition? (Why not try it with your people?)

Will you begin to capitalise on this free powerful lever to producing greater employee performance?

CHAPTER 12

Creating A Sense Of Fun In Your Organisation To Enable High Performance

WORK MADE FUN GETS DONE BETTER

"Work is a big part of all of our lives, and there is no point in working somewhere that has no sense of enjoyment or fun. We spend a large chunk of our lives in work, so you don't want to be somewhere that makes you miserable or unhappy. The very best employees are the ones who can create the right atmosphere, but at the same time remain highly productive. Culture is not just about Christmas parties & fun days out – it's about people at the top being open to ideas from everyone – this is a great motivator & shows people how valued they are." James Caan Entrepreneur

"A business has to be involving, it has to be fun, and it has to exercise your creative instincts." Richard Branson

"Make work fun," Jody Urqhart

"Work made fun gets done better." Mike Kerr

> "Fun is one of the most important – and under-rated – ingredients of any successful venture. If you're not having fun, then it's probably time to call it quits & try something else." Richard Branson

THE 'PROFESSIONALISATION' OF WORK CAN BE AWFULLY DULL!

I was always taught not to take myself too seriously, since it would inhibit my effectiveness. I believe the same to be true about the workplace itself.

Too many organisations have allowed work to become procedural, rule bound and dull. They prefer process over personality, and in doing so have cut down on flair, enthusiasm and creativity.

Is your own workplace dull, or do your people have fun at work? Is your workplace operating at a higher level of performance because your people really enjoy what they are doing? Is there a vibrancy about the workplace, and do your teams have fun whilst working together?

This really matters.................is fun 'allowed' in your workplace, or has it been driven out by serious people who take everything seriously?

RICHARD BRANSON IS A COMMITTED DEVOTEE OF FUN AND LAUGHTER IN THE WORKPLACE

In the same way that Richard Branson devotes 25% of his book 'The Virgin Way' to listening...........he also spends a third of that book talking about the importance of fun and laughing at work.

You could say that Richard and the Virgin organisation take 'fun' very seriously indeed. If the workplace is somewhere that most working adults spend half of their week.............and if it is not an environment in which to enjoy spontaneous good times.....then it is fair to ask...."what is the point of it all?" If work is miserable or dull (or both)...........then life is pretty much made miserable. It cannot be erased by a few hours in the evening and a weekend off!

Richard Branson believes that a sense of humour, and the ability not to take ourselves too seriously, are both crucially important attributes to any healthy corporate culture.

Richard's people get an amazing 'buzz' talking to their friends about "the crazy things we do at Virgin". Virgin, very much like Google, is inundated with job applications from great people, who are desperate to go and do work in a 'fun' culture. Fun at work is brand enhancing. Fun at work widens your great candidate pool. It's also life enhancing...............fun is definitely good for personal wellbeing.

If your own team members are engaged, having fun, and genuinely care about people..............they will enjoy their work and do a better job. It really is that simple. This is not a complex concept. Ask yourself the question..................Does that describe your workplace culture? Is it really a fun place to work?

JOHN ROBERTS AT AO.COM HAS EXACTLY THE SAME PHILOSOPHY AS RICHARD BRANSON – FUNNY ISN'T IT?

I've already cited John Roberts, CEO of DRL/AO.com, who has done very well in the Best Companies league in recent years, and runs a business with a great culture. John's philosophy is identical to that of Richard Branson, in the context of fun in the workplace.

John told me that his philosophy is that we spend so much of our life at work, that it needs to be enjoyable. How we are in our workplace carries over into our daily lives. He firmly believes that his people should be happy at work, so that they can sound happy over the phone to customers.

The AO.com maxim is to treat every customer as if it were your Gran. Their call centres have no prescriptions/no scripts, just a requirement for a voice which sounds happy. It is very difficult, in reality, to sound happy if you are not happy in your work in the first place.

John Roberts encourages his people to have fun with customers. Fun in the team has an authentic way of leaking out into behaviour with customers. You cannot really fake this sort of thing. Customers can tell whether you are behaving by wrote and talking to a set script...........or whether you are authentically happy to help them. We humans are pretty perceptive............ and a happy workplace is infectious in making everyone feel better.

I wonder if your customers can tell you whether they think your people are having fun at work?

HOW HAPPY ARE YOUR PEOPLE? ARE YOU NURTURING A FUN PLACE TO WORK?

Jeffrey Pfeffer's book 'the Human Equation', asserts that the challenge for all business leaders is "creating a fun; challenging and empowered work environment in which individuals are able to use their abilities to do meaningful jobs; for which they are shown appreciation, to enhance motivation and performance."

Professor Cary Cooper, of Lancaster University Business School, believes that the 'penny may have dropped' for many CEOs, since they are beginning to give thought to the creation of a happier place to work, in order to have a direct and positive impact on their bottom line.

Indeed, research studies by Harvard Business School have shown a causal link between happiness at work and productivity in the workplace. Happiness is a fuel for success. There is no doubt, research shows that your brain.....when positive.....performs significantly better than when you are negative or stressed. Your intelligence and energy levels rise......in short....you are both more resilient and more productive.

If you are an enlightened executive/leader/CEO, then the happiness of your workforce, and the fun elements required to achieve that feeling, should be a key objective for you. Are you working on the fun factor in your organisation? How good are the levels of happiness in your own workforce?

According to a 2010 study, only 45% of people are happy at work. That has to mean that over half the colleagues you meet actually don't want to be at their work, because they are not happy doing it!! That's a shocking statistic. It says to me that any great leader needs to realise the power of fun, and has to be working on creating that happy and productive working atmosphere which employees will love...................and productivity will rise.

THIRD SECTOR EMPLOYEES ARE THE HAPPIEST AT WORK – THERE MUST BE SOMETHING ABOUT PURPOSE IN CAUSING THIS

A 2016 study, for the British Household panel survey, showed there is a significant positive impact on life satisfaction (happiness and fun) from working in the third sector/for a non-profit organisation.

Another study, by Bard College Berlin Professor Martin Binder, estimated that the happiness derived from third sector jobs was roughly equivalent to a salary increase of £22,000 per annum. Martin Binder attributed the findings to the increased enjoyment of day to day activities in the third sector, purely because those people had a strong feeling of inherent usefulness. They felt that what they were doing was really worthwhile.

Why do people work in a voluntary capacity without payment? It is due to a strong sense of purpose.

You may not have a life-saving purpose, as some third sector organisations do..........but you can certainly think about whether your sense of purpose is more than just the creation of profit. Clearly profitability is important, but it does need to combine with an overarching purpose which has meaning for employees. Purpose definitely impacts upon the happiness and wellbeing of your people, and merits serious thought.

PRÉT A MANGER – A HAPPY PLACE FOR CUSTOMERS (WITHOUT THIRD SECTOR TYPE PURPOSE)

Businesses who do not have that 'worthwhile mission' of the third sector, can achieve purpose in a fun, happy and productive workplace.

Prét a Manger have a really strong fun culture. Prét baristas are told that they can give free coffees to anyone they like as part of their work. Prét employees get a buzz from this bit of fun, and customers do too. Many of these little 'fun' things that Prét do, combine to make a fun and happy place to work.

Prét also gives away free sandwiches and other food at the end of every day........to homeless people. This is a simple act, which fulfils the 'freshly made every day' tagline.......but makes employees......and customers feel happy about the way the business operates.

I guess Prét employees talk to their families about who they have given free coffees away to, and about how their business gives free food to homeless people to avoid waste, and preserve freshness every day. This kind of action leads to a fun, happy and highly motivated workforce.................who have a sense of purpose around freshness......and the vitality of spontaneous gifting.

Fun is a tangible productivity factor..........and tricky though that may be.....I am challenging you to think about how you can work on that 'feel-good' factor.

SUMMARY POINTS:

- Work made fun gets done better
- Is your workplace professional but dull? What do your people say about it?
- Are you 'Branson-like' and a believer in the power of fun and laughter to generate better work outcomes?
- Is the culture at your organisation fun and desirable? Does your fun culture widen your recruitment candidate pool? Are good people queuing up to work for you? If not, why not?
- Are you working on enhancing fun and happiness in your workplace?
- Have you created a sense of purpose in the work your people do which is more than just profitability?

YOUR ACTIONS:

What will you do next about fun in your workplace?

Can you identify an overarching purpose which will make your people realise that their work really matters?

CHAPTER 13

Reperesenting 'The Cynics' –
On Culture And Engagement

**THERE ARE THOSE WHO WOULD DISPUTE THE
POWER OF ENGAGING YOUR PEOPLE**

"I am most proud of my integrity, and least proud
of my cynicism." Chloe Sevigny

"Remember, you cannot be both young and wise.
Young people who pretend to be wise to the ways
of the world are mostly just cynics. Cynicism mas-
querades as wisdom, but is the farthest thing from
it. Because cynics don't learn anything. Cynicism is
a self-imposed blindness, a rejection of the world,
because we think it will hurt or disappoint us.
Cynics always say "no". But saying "yes" begins
things. Saying "yes" leads to knowledge. So for as
long as you have the strength to; say "yes".
Stephen Colbert

"Cynicism is like folding your arms, stepping
back & commenting on things, like the old guys
in 'the Muppets'; just throwing out comments all
the time. Whereas, there are other people on the

ground really trying to affect things, improve their lives, and the lives of other people. I think that is noble & cool." Josh Radnor

"I think too often we make choices, based on the safety of cynicism, and what we're led to is a life not fully lived. Cynicism is fear, and it's worse than fear, it's active disengagement." Ken Burns

ACADEMICS AND OTHERS ARE OFTEN CYNICAL AND 'SQUEAMISH' ABOUT ENGAGEMENT AND PERFORMANCE

I would be remiss in this book, if I did not represent the views of the cynics about the power of engagement and the link to performance.

The cynics cite the fact that the engagement surveys being 'peddled' by various consultancies are somewhat 'dodgy'..........that is certainly true. Beware what you are buying..........and from whom you are buying into your business to run such surveys. There are too many people in the marketplace who are surfing the wave of interest in engagement and culture, who will run you a survey, leave you with a load of impenetrable data, and very little else. This is clearly not a solution I would recommend. Surveys are not the essence of culture – and are not the end – they are merely a means to an end which must be used carefully.

The cynics would also hold the view that there is no measurable state which, when achieved, can result in greater performance.......forever.

I would agree that those in the engagement movement, have made some pretty wild claims...........and that needs to be seen as nonsense. It's a good thing to jettison the claims of the more outrageous purveyors out there. As I said..............beware whom you work with!!

There are new ideas and concepts which emerge, from time to time..............some of which have a sound empirical base.......whilst others rely more on marketing hype (often by consulting businesses who want to give their models compelling selling attraction) to give them 'legs'.

The academics feel it is too soon to tell whether engaging your people will give sustainable productivity gains over the long term, or whether this is merely a passing 'fad' of business and culture. Their concern is around whether this will become a long term established part of accepted management best practice.

As a practitioner myself, I have long nailed my personal colours firmly to the mast. I am a believer in the concept of engagement and driving a positive culture. I have cited for the reader, and seen a lot of real on the ground evidence that there is something in this whole business ....and that 'culture really does trump strategy'. You will no doubt make up your own mind.

Academia is still very much divided, and will no doubt spend some many years gathering more evidence, and debating topics in this whole arena. My view would be that practitioners should get on with building cultures which perform at a higher level than the competitive set, and leave the theory to catch you up!!

THE GOVERNMENT VIEW FOR ENGAGING EMPLOYEES AND THE LINK TO PERFORMANCE

Business culture, the need to engage people to improve performance, and the general belief in causal links..............has historically received cross-party political support in successive U.K. governments. Lord Mandelson, in the Labour administration of 2008, set up the MacLeod review, to explore the potential of employee engagement..............in order to improve U.K. productivity and competitiveness. The resulting MacLeod report, published in 2009, strongly supported the concept of a causal link between culture, engagement and productivity.

The MacLeod report was subsequently endorsed in the Conservative administration of David Cameron. This then led to the setting up of a Task Force of leading industrialists, to promote the concept of an 'engagement movement', using the moniker of 'Engage for Success'.

Is cross-party political support the 'kiss of death', or is it a recognition by all political persuasions that there is something tangible to be gained in productivity by having a culture in which people are positive and engaged?

The Conservative government of David Cameron, was also interested in the topic of positive psychology at work. Work & organisational psychologists have expressed a growing interest, within academic research, in the effects of positive psychology in the workplace. There has been a regular National survey commissioned by the then Prime Minister on the subject of happiness. Some views on social media expressed cynical derision of this survey, whilst others have taken the topic very seriously........as a topic which contributed to national productivity.

Again, you must observe, make choices, and act accordingly. I can only make my own case for a belief that the way your employees 'feel' will affect their performance............and leave the cynics out there to catch up. In my own view.......culture definitely counts massively.

WHAT ARE THE CAUSES OF CYNICISM & CONCERN AROUND CAUSAL LINKS BETWEEN ENGAGEMENT & PERFORMANCE?

The biggest issue that both cynics and academics cite is what they term 'causality'. There have been too few studies over time, which seek to alter engagement levels and test the effects. Academics hold the view that such studies are urgently needed.

Another area of concern, is whether too much engagement and stimulus could cause 'burn out'? Engagement was originally seen as enhancing workplace culture, to combat traditional burn out, but some would argue that too much engagement with the workplace culture could be a negative factor?

There is also much argument about what organisational engagement actually is. The CIPD defined it as: 'a combination of commitment to the organisation & its values, and a willingness to help our colleagues/organisational citizenship. It goes beyond job satisfaction, and is not simply motivation. Engagement is something the employee has to offer; it cannot be required as part of the employment contract.' (CIPD 2012). I like this definition, because it gets to the heart of the fact that employees only give discretionary effort, when they really believe in the values of the organisation and a transcending purpose.

The MacLeod review definition of engagement is 'a workplace approach, designed to ensure that employees are committed to their organisation's goal & values, motivated to contribute to organisational success, and are able at the same time to enhance their own wellbeing'. This definition is helpful for me, in emphasising that a great culture is not just more productive, it is good for you as a person...............a great place to work.

Not only do the cynics have a problem with definitions, they express concerns about measurement. There are, as has already been mentioned, multiple measurement surveys for engagement and culture. In addition to the previously referenced and most famous Gallup Q12, there are tools from the likes of Aon Hewitt; Hay; Kenexa; Towers-Watson and many less well-known others. All are developing and selling their own particular measures of culture, morale and engagement in organisations.

This plethora of surveys, leads academics in particular to have concerns around a lack of reasons for including or excluding individual questions in survey formats.

Into the melee of opinion, the 'Engage for Success' task force commissioned a review of the evidence concerning the impact of engagement on performance............and other factors.....in 2012. The review concluded that there was convincing evidence that high levels of engagement do deliver strong bottom-line effects to organisations. Their conclusion was..........culture counts.

It has to also be mentioned, that the cynics view is that the 2012 report did not properly define engagement; it did not specify how engagement should best be measured; and it was said that claims by organisations to have gained significant financial outcomes by engaging their people were too readily accepted, without question.

My own view, is that whilst many of these criticsms have some validity..........there is sufficient [evidence] in the concept of how people feel about their organisation; the people who lead them; and the mission/purpose/values they believe in........will impact performance.......either positively or negatively. As a practitioner, I'm not looking for a scientific formula, I'm looking for practical pointers to what I can do to improve business performance.....and I have lived through sufficient business turnaround experience, and talked to enough CEOs to know that culture really does trump strategy.

Every executive I speak to...............I ask the question "how much do you think culture affects performance?"

.............and as I said earlier they always answer with the same word.........."massively".

I wonder what you think, as the reader, about the views of the cynics around this subject?

DO PEOPLE WANT TO BE ENGAGED AT WORK?

The cynics would hold the view that not everybody wants to be 'engaged' at work. Some people see work as purely transactional......'a fair day's work for a fair day's pay' and then they go home. There are people in any population that would hold that view.

There are some individuals whose whole work orientation is to demonstrate a loathing of their place of work. Indeed, they seem to get a kick out of hating the system they work in. I guess we have all come across a few people like that in our time!

Other individuals may say, somewhat cynically, that all this talk of building culture and engagement is a one-way street...........purely for the benefit of the organisation...........a kind of mass manipulation of your people.

The cynics would say – "what is in this for the employee?" My retort would be that I would far rather work in an organisation that sets out to enthuse and engage me; to lead me in such a way that I feel 'in the loop' about what is going on in my business; that people listen to my views; and recognise my contributions...........it is bound to be more enjoyable for me as the employee. If that enhances productivity for the organisation.............it will simultaneously provide me with the satisfaction of a vibrant & motivational place to work..........far better than a dull and procedural workplace................and it will also be successful in giving me job security and financial rewards commensurate with the type of work I do.

If I feel motivated and engaged as an employee, surely I will be more likely to give freely of my discretionary effort..........and ultimately that more productive business will then be able to give me a share of the overall success. Isn't that what Maslow was talking about in the 1950s, when he talked about self- actualisation?

HOW TO ENGAGE AND BUILD A CULTURE IS REGARDED AS BEING UNCLEAR

The final criticism of the cynics, is that there is no clear 'programme' of what you need to do to enhance engagement and build a strong culture.

I see so many organisations setting off down the road of employing a consultancy to conduct an attitude/engagement survey for them. They then seek to benchmark results and take appropriate action. Whilst this may well be a starting point, for many it is too vague, and not precise regarding actions and effective intervention.

This book has been written in order to illustrate, by stories and cases, some principles and examples of what strong positive cultures (who employ highly engaged people) have done in the real world.

Clearly, customisation to a company's strengths and weaknesses is a critical factor..............but there are sufficient examples in this book of the things which work in real businesses...........and have a positive effect upon performance............that it must make it easier for an executive to figure out what they need to do on a practical level.

BEWARE THOSE PEDDLING ADVICE IN THIS WHOLE AREA OF ENGAGEMENT AND CULTURE

Because 'employee engagement' has become an extremely popular and topical concept, many people have flooded into the marketplace selling advice.

Before you embark on work to enhance you culture ....seeking to engage your people..........with a view to improve the performance of your business ....choose very carefully whom you use. Select assistance and advice from practitioners with a track record of having achieved improvements in this area in real world businesses. Those who have genuinely taken the knocks of failure, and seen the highs of success will be of most practical use to your business. They will be the ones who really know what they are talking about, because what they have done previously in actual organisations, really has worked.

Be suitably dubious about anyone selling an engagement survey who has never worked in a real life business situation.

SUMMARY POINTS:

- Are you a cynic who will doubt the effectiveness of seeking to engage your people? (or are you someone who will say "yes – I need to give this a go"?)
- Does the fact that the U.K. government has invested into wellbeing at work influence you...... or put you off?
- What do you think about your people? Are they sufficiently engaged? Could you do more?
- Has this book given you a clear link to what builds culture and engages people?
- Have you got the right advice to be able to devise your own customised programme and move forward?

YOUR ACTIONS:

Will you sit with the cynics and require more proof about the link between productivity and engagement?

Do you buy into the concept that culture trumps strategy..........and you want to start work on it?

CHAPTER 14

Culture And Performance Is Not A Quick Fix – But The Journey Is An Important One

LEADERS NEED TO BE WORKING ON THE CULTURE

"Culture eats strategy for breakfast" Peter Drucker

THE CIPD's VIEW ON THE IMPORTANCE OF CULTURE

I have been a member of the CIPD (my professional body) for over 40 years. I hold the most senior rank of companion of the chartered institute, and have long respected the research work they undertake.

I want to commence my final chapter with one such piece of CIPD research............a report from 2016 entitled 'a duty to care – evidence of the importance of organisational culture to effective governance and leadership.' The report was compiled in conjunction with the Financial Reporting Council. I am including here a piece from the foreword to that report, written by Peter Cheese, the Chief Executive of the CIPD:

"Healthy and positive organisation cultures matter. Culture is integral to organisational success, and to the well-being of our workforces. Numerous highly public corporate scandals, most of which were rooted in poor or poorly aligned organisational cultures, have put culture in the spotlight once and for all.

Changing or creating good workplace cultures is not an exact science, it takes time, and is influenced by many variables. Leaders think they know what the culture is, but rarely fully understand it.

Many researchers talk about positive attributes of culture or high performing cultures, but cutting and pasting the success of others may not achieve the desired result. Creating effective culture starts with recognising just how crucial employees are to the success of our organisations. Leaders need to recognise that every decision they make for their organisation, has an important people dimension.

People provide knowledge, ideas & sparks of innovation that deliver value for the business – and can deliver competitive advantage. When cultures turn toxic; trust breaks down, and both performance and well-being suffer. The damage is often irreparable – not just in terms of financial value – or the response of customers who often vote with their feet – but also in terms of staff engagement & the health of the workforce.

Boards have a duty to understand the cultures of their organisations, and to invest in creating the best environment they can, for people to perform – aligned to the goals of the enterprise."

I must say, I couldn't have put this better – or indeed more eloquently myself...........and I could not agree more with Peter's words. The CIPD is working in conjunction with the Financial Reporting council's culture coalition, to recommend that Boards of companies take full account of the culture of the organisation......and take evidence based steps.......evaluating, understanding, measuring and managing the culture of their businesses. It is a Board's responsibility to understand the culture of the organisation, how it is changing, and holding management to account.

Culture is complex, and the Board/leadership team must understand it and manage it. Leadership needs to develop trust through frequent communication.......and dialogue with the workforce........giving employees real voice (my principles: communicate; communicate; communicate – and regular systematic listening resonate). Also key is hiring people who fit the culture (hire for attitude) and managing performance (deal with your underperformers and push your talent)............ all these principles are highlighted in the CIPD/FRC 2016 report.

This influential 2016 report serves to endorse all the principles I have been illustrating and exemplifying, for you the reader, in this book. As Peter Drucker said "Culture eats strategy for breakfast."

A FINANCIAL LONG TERM ANALYSIS OF THE 'WORTH' OF BUSINESS CULTURE

Alex Edmans, Professor of Finance at the London Business School, presented a paper at the 'Engage or bust' conference (for David MacLeod and his team) in November 2015. His paper was entitled (not exactly snappily); 'the link between job satisfaction and firm value, with implications for corporate social responsibility.'

Alex Edmans' findings were that companies listed in the 100 Best Companies to work for in America index generated 2.3-3.8% higher stock returns per year, than their peers from 1984 through to 2011. He used the finance literature methodology...........looking at firm level value, and found job satisfaction to be valuable to that macro-level indicator.

His findings indicated that job satisfaction causes stronger corporate performance, and that corporate social responsibility can improve stock returns. He warns that this only happens in the long run. There is a time lag shown in Alex Edmans analysis between achieving job satisfaction in the enterprise, and this value appearing in the stock market. He also points out that it takes time for managerial actions to feed through into job satisfaction in the workforce.

I agree with Professor Edmans that culture is a long term slog. That long slog is not for the faint hearted...........but the rewards for the people employed and also for the success of the enterprise are there for the taking. I'm still fully with Drucker that "Culture eats strategy for breakfast," even if that is shown over the long haul.

WHAT IS IN THIS FOR THE EMPLOYEES?

I have presented a lot of evidence that a great place to work, and a positive culture, will enhance performance and shareholder value.

For me, the case for the employee is equally straightforward and compelling. It is better to work in a place where the employee believes in the mission/purpose and values of the enterprise. This is especially true when that mission transcends merely making money (despite the fact that commercial success provides the revenue for the income paid to employees – a fairly obvious but often overlooked point). People seek meaning and purpose in what they are doing in work. They give ideas, innovation and discretionary effort when they believe in the higher purpose of the organisation.

When experiencing leadership, employees admire communication which inspires them and being given voice through a management which listens to feedback............these are the elements of a place people will want to work in, and which gives them job satisfaction & fulfilment. Couple this with an environment where employees are recognised for a job well done, and the place they work has a sense of fun............... and individuals are going to feel the benefit of a great place to work. The fact this enhances productivity and shareholder value is only part of the equation ....the value to employees is that sense of pride in the business, loyalty to a cause and a sense of well-being.

WHAT ARE YOU GOING TO DO DIFFERENTLY AS A RESULT OF READING 'CULTURE TRUMPS STRATEGY'?

I've really enjoyed writing this book. I've gained great satisfaction talking to CEOs of businesses who believe

in building great cultures. I have also enjoying research-
ing the link between culture, engagement of employees
and high performance.

The thing which has stuck me most in this piece of
work, is the amazing commonality of the threads/initia-
tives/actions in the many business sectors...................
concerning 'hiring for attitude'; inspiring communication; employee voice; fun and recognition. These
themes recur because they are common to the human
condition.

I think that the 21st century workplace will continue to
change. Technology will continue to enable and facili-
tate...but also present new challenges. Work will continue to be done from multiple locations, in the home
and in the office...........and in the high street coffee
shop. Flexible approaches to ways of working will also
continue to adapt to these changing parameters. The
fact remains that people will still be human, with similar
needs for recognition; inspiration and a sense of voice.
The generations coming along into the workplace will
continue to be better educated, and more demanding of
employers and leadership in the workplace.

Those CEOs and employers who 'grasp the nettle' in
creating a purpose for employees which transcends
money, and develop a culture which is famous for being
a great place to work, will be the ones who will win out
over the long term.

I know that this cultural agenda is a worthwhile
quest..........and I hope you the reader, have reached a

similar conclusion & caught the vision. I wish you well in leading your organisation, and I trust this book has proved thought provoking..............and has given you some clear actions to take back into your workplace. I hope I have also given you warning of some of the classic traps of simplistic solutions which some businesses fall into. Don't be the CEO who thinks morale has improved, just because you changed your survey measurements. Don't be the executive whose culture results were so bad that the survey went into a desk drawer, never to see the light of day again.

The very best CEOs, and leaders of organisations are alive to the fact that culture really does trump strategy. They would rather lead in an enlightened way, to produce the culture of a great place to work............. giving job satisfaction to their employees...........and subsequently reap the long term rewards – than go for short term objectives which don't establish a good healthy organisation. I trust you are inspired to become that kind of leader.

SUMMARY POINTS:

- Do you agree that culture is integral to organisational success?
- Does your Board take seriously the responsibility for investing into creating the best environment for your people to perform?
- Do you understand that the inputs to building a strong culture take time to achieve – this is not a quick-fix?
- Do you accept that shareholder value and high performance will only be demonstrated in the long run?
- Do you realise that this is about creating a great place to work, in order to create pride/fulfilment & motivation for your people?

YOUR ACTIONS:

Are you going to take action...................along with your top team, to build a customised plan to enhance/create a high performance culture in your own organisation?

Lightning Source UK Ltd.
Milton Keynes UK
UKOW02f1640121216
289806UK00001B/8/P